Books to Bullets . . . In Defiance of Northern Propaganda!

A History of the 46th North Carolina Infantry, CSA

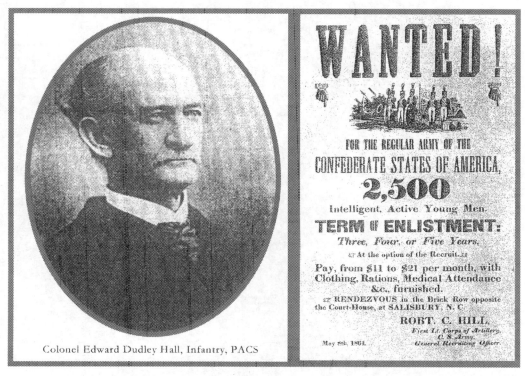

Colonel Edward Dudley Hall, Infantry, PACS

(Excerpts from the Civil War Memoirs of the officers and men of the 46th North Carolina Infantry Regiment, State Troops, C. S. A.)

COL Charles W. L. Hall, Ph.D.

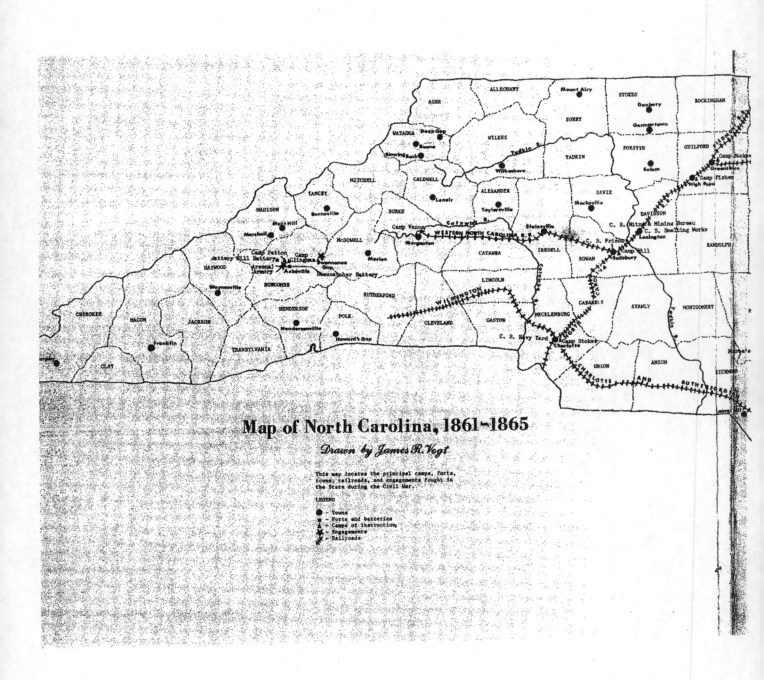

Map of North Carolina, 1861–1865

Drawn by James R. Vogt

This map locates the principal camps, forts,
towns, railroads, and engagements fought in
the State during the Civil War.

LEGEND

- = Towns
- = Forts and batteries
- = Camps of instruction
- = Engagements
- = Railroads

War for Southern Independence

STATE OF NORTH CAROLINA – 1860

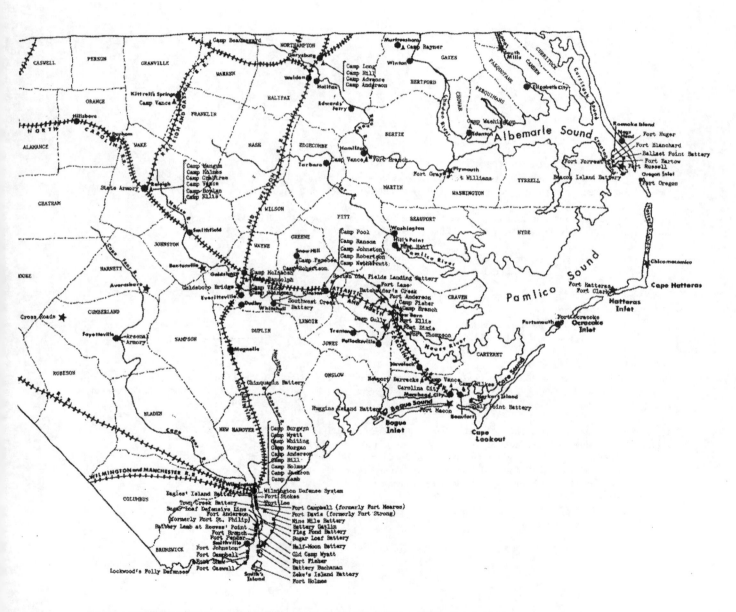

RE: NORTH CAROLINA STATE TROOPS

M-1

Order this book online at www.trafford.com
or email orders@trafford.com

Most Trafford titles are also available at major online book retailers.

In respect for the scholarship contained herein, the acid-free paper used in this book meets the guidelines for permanence and durability of the Committee on Production Guidelines for book Longevity of the Council on Library Resources.

For a complete list of available publications:
New Horizons Development Co. Ltd.
Post Office Box 15171
Hattiesburg, NS 39404-1517 USA

All Maps and Tables published with the authorization of
A Prentice-Hall Macmillan Company, New York, NY.

Hall, Edward Dudley, b.1823 d.1896.
Bibles to Bullets-in the defiance of Northern Propaganda: a history of the 46th Regiment North Carolina Infantry CSA: the Civil War memories and diary entries of the men of the 46th North Carolina Regiment / complied and edited by COL Charles W.L. Hall, Ph.D. p. cm.
Includes bibliographical references and index. (Acid free paper available)

1. Confederate States of America. Army. North Carolina Infantry Regiment, 46th.
2. United States—History—Civil War, 1861-1865—Regimental histories.
3. North Carolina—History—Civil War, 1860-1865—Regimental histories.
4. United States—History—Civil War, 1861-1865—Personal narratives, Confederate.
5. North Carolina—History—Civil War, 1861-1865—Personal narratives.
6. Hall, Edward Dudley b. 1823—Diary.
7. Soldiers—North Carolina—New Hanover County—Diary. I. Hall, Charles W.L., 1946-. II Titles.
    E573.3 M3 973.74—' 00-00000

Printed in the United States of America.

ISBN: 978-1-4669-1282-3 (sc)
ISBN: 978-1-4669-1281-6 (e)

Trafford rev. 04/02/2013

North America & International
toll-free: 1 888 232 4444 (USA & Canada)
phone: 250 383 6864 ♦ fax: 812 355 4082

BOOKS
TO
BULLETS...

IN

DEFIANCE OF
NORTHERN PROPAGANDA!

HISTORY

OF THE

FORTY-SIXTH REGIMENT

NORTH CAROLINA INFANTRY
(STATE TROOPS)

IN THE

WAR FOR SOUTHERN INDEPENDENCE

Complied and Edited By:

COL CHARLES W.L. HALL, Ph.D.
Confederate Historian

WANTED!

FOR THE REGULAR ARMY OF THE
CONFEDERATE STATES OF AMERICA,

2,500

Intelligent, Active Young Men.

TERM OF ENLISTMENT:

Three, Four, or Five Years,

At the option of the Recruit.

Pay, from \$11 to \$21 per month, with Clothing, Rations, Medical Attendance &c., furnished.

RENDEZVOUS in the Brick Row opposite the Court-House, at SALISBURY, N. C.

ROBT. C. HILL,

First Lt. Corps of Artillery,
C. S. Army,
General Recruiting Officer.

May 8th, 1861.

ISBN 0-86526-006-0 (Volume I)
ISBN 0-86526-005-2 (Set)

This story is a **memorial** to the men, and their yet
untold story of devotion and sacrifice in
Following units:

Manning's Brigade
Walker's Division
Longstreet's Corps

Cooke's Brigade
Ransom's Division
Third Mil Dist, Dept SC/GA/FL;

Cooke's Brigade
Heth's Division
A.P. Hill's (Early's) Corps;

TROOPS OF NORTH CAROLINA
Department of North Carolina
(Staging Area)

ARMY OF NORTHERN VIRGINIA, CSA
(Field Operations)
General Robert Edward Lee
General-in-Chief, C.S.A.

CONTENTS

Appendicies

About the Author

Colonel Charles W.L. Hall, Ph.D. is an Educator, Psychologist and Minister and a longtime resident of Mississippi; a Confederate Historian, by being a practical student of the War for Southern Independence for over fifty years. His Great-grandfather an officer of the 46th North Carolina Infantry Regiment; Himself, past commander of Camp #1329, SCV; and awarded the War Service Cross by the UDC; and the Southern Cross by the OSC, for his preservation efforts on the Franklin Battlefield Restoration. COL Hall, a career officer of the U.S. Army's Adjutant General Corps, and a war veteran of the Cold War, Vietnam War and the Gulf War – retiring with over thirty years service. He has used both his academic training and military experience to bring this Confederate Regiment back to life. A.A.G.

Dedications

&

Memories . . .

In preservation of my children's southern heritage . . .
and,
the challenge of my cousin Dale Greenwell, in his successful writing of the
3rd Mississippi Infantry;

In the memory of my dear friend, mentor, compatriot and scholar

The late

Major-General William D. McCain, US Army. Retired.
Adjutant-in-Chief, Sons of Confederate Veterans;

and

My fellow friends & compatriots of the

Sons of Conderate Veterans
Headquarters Camp # 584
1972-2006;

The Confederate Veterans, ladies and children
of **the Great State of Mississippi.**

and

In the memory of our beloved

Confederacy . . . !

War for Southern Independence

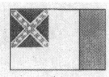

Traditional
"REGIMENTAL COLORS with HONORS"
Forty-Sixth North Carolina Infantry of Volunteers
4 April 1862 - 9 April 1865

Symbols of the Confederate Army in the Field
"Army of North Virginia"

"Jackson's Corps" "The Battle Flag" "Longstreet's Corps"

46th Regiment North Carolina Infantry Volunteers

Military Campaign Credits, 1861-1865:

I.   BATTLE OF MALVERN HILL (VA)

II.   BATTLE OF SHARPSBURG (MD)

III.   BATTLE OF FREDERICKSBURG (VA)

IV.   BATTLE OF BRISTOE STATION (VA)

V.   BATTLE OF WILDERNESS (VA)

VI.   BATTLE OF SPOTSYLANIA (VA)

VII.   BATTLE OF COLD HARBOR (VA)

VIII.   BATTLE OF RICHMOND (VA)

IX.   BATTLE OF PETERSBURG (VA)

1862 Army of N. Virginia	1863 Army of N. Virginia	1864 Army of N. Virginia
Longstreet's I Corps	Third Mil Dist, Dept SC/GA/FL	A.P. Hill's (Early)Corps
Walker's Division	Ransom's Division	Heth's Division
Manning Brigade	Cooke's Brigade	Cooke's Brigade

FORTY-SIXTH NORTH CAROLINA INFANTRY of VOLUNTEERS
Field and Staff—Headquarters, Camp Mangum, Raleigh, N.C.

<u>Colonel Edward Dudley Hall (4Apr62), Commander***</u>
<u>*Lieutenant-Colonel William A. Jenkins (4Apr62)</u>
<u>*Major Rush J. Mitchell (4Apr62)</u>

COMPANY "A" "Lumberton Guards"
*Captain Richard M. Norment (4Apr62) County

COMPANY "B" "Rifles"
*Captain William L. Saunders (4Apr62) County

COMPANY "C" "Rifles"
*Captain Stephen W. Jones (4Apr62) County

COMPANY "D" "Sons of Mars"
*Captain Colin Stewart (4Apr62) County

COMPANY "E" "Tar River Rebels"
*Captain Robert L. Heflin (4Apr62) County

COMPANY "F" "Rifles"
*Captain Alex C. McAlister (4Apr62) County

COMPANY "G" "Randolph Rangers"
*Captain Obed William Carr (4Apr62) County

COMPANY "H" "Moore Guards"
Captain Neill McKay McNeill (4Apr62) County**

COMPANY "I" "Coharie Guards"
Captain Owen Holmes (4Apr62) County**

COMPANY "K" "Catawba Braves"
Captain Adolphus T. Bost (4Apr62) County ?

* killed   Transferred ***   resigned **

Captain in 1861, and soon rose to the rank of Colonel. As Commander of the Forty-sixth North Carolina Infantry, he honored his grand old State.

EDWARD DUDLEY HALL
Brigadier – General
Provisional Army of the Confederate States

Unit of Assignment
Cooke's Brigade
Heth's Division
P. Hill's (III) Corps
Army of Northern Virginia

Record of Advancement
Organized:
* New Hanover Irish "Rifle Ranges" Artillery Company
Enlisted:
Private, * Company H/ 3rd N.C. Artillery
Commissioned:
Captain, Company A, 2nd N.C. Regt. State Troops
Major, Adjutant, F&S, 7th N.C. Regt. State Troops
Colonel, Commanding, * 46th N.C. Vol. Regt., CSA

Salutes
Cited for Personal Bravery at the Battle of New Bern, N.C.
Cited for Heroic Charge at the Battle of Sharpsburg
Participated in 13 Battles across N.C., VA., and MD.

Citizen-Soldier
Legislature of North Carolina
New Hanover County Sheriff
State Senator of North Carolina
Mayor of City of Wilmington
Nominated State Lt-Governor
Major-General of the United Confederate Veterans, N.C.
b. 1823 m. Sallie Landon Green d. 11 June 1896

Forty-sixth Regiment N.C. Troops: (1) Colonel William L. Saunders; (2) Lieutenant Colonel Alexander C. McAllister; (3) Captain Robert A. Bost, Company K; (4) Captain Robert Preston Troy, Company G; (5) Captain Jesse Franklin Heflin, Company E; (6) Captain Obed William Carr, Company G; and (7) Captain Adolphus Theodrous Bost, Company K. Original photograph appears in Volume III of *Histories of the Several Regiments and Battalions from North Carolina in the Great War 1861-'65*, edited by Walter Clark.

INTRODUCTION

There are no more survivors of the Forty-Sixth North Carolina volunteers (the Regiment thereof). Their heroic deeds and adventurous exploits have been buried in the archives and libraries of last resort, much like the "volunteers in gray" who were interned along the dusty roads and byways across the battlefields of the Southern Confederacy, a legacy paved in victories, defeats, and finally in surrender! They returned home beaten and wore on the outside, but victorious on the inside from a higher morale plain of satisfaction—knowing that they had given there very best, and yet, they had served honorable, but in their mind they remained un-surrendered in their cause.

I the author have been interested in the War for Southern Independence since I was a young child, that interest was reinforced by the excitement of the Centennial 1960-1965, and finally brought to fruitarian through my own family's genealogical research. My interest in the Forty-Sixth Regiment of North Carolina Volunteers (Infantry), was crystallized when the late President-Major General William D. McCain, University of Southern Mississippi, ask me to form a Son's of Confederate Veterans camp in Hattiesburg, Mississippi (a camp had not existed here since the 1950's).

In 1974, General McCain was serving also as the Adjutant-in-Chief, Son's of Confederate Veterans, headquartered at USM, and operated the Mississippi Division, Headquarters Camp #584 (of which I was a member in good standing since being credentialed in December 1972, while serving in the United States Army at Fort Ord, California).

I thought it a challenge and undertook to raise the Hattiesburg SCV Camp #1329. Prior to the actual chartering of the Camp, I had set about to learn our local history. I had been aware of my own Confederate ancestry for a long time. The Hall family migrated from England to Virginia in 1730. The family finally moved to North Carolina in the early 1800's. In 1861 my Great Grandfather Edward Dudley Hall while serving as County Sheriff, funded the organizing of a Company of Artillery, called the "Wilmington Irish."

While researching the Confederate Archives at USM, the State Archives in Jackson and the State Archives in Raleigh, I further discovered that an infantry company had been organized of the men in New Hanover County of the City of Wilmington. The unit was known as Company "A" and composed chiefly of local Irishmen, and their first elected commander—Captain Edward Dudley Hall on March 1861, and accepted for state service.

During the month of May 1861, the North Carolina State Legislature passed an act, for the creation of North Carolina military forces. Early recruitment was under taken by the state militia and patriotic citizens. Later a new regiment would eventually be formed from southeastern counties of Robeson, Rowan, Burke, Warren, Richmond, Granville, Moore, Randolph, Sampson and Catawba of North Carolina, and to be trained in camp at Magnum in the spring of '61, to be known as the 46th North Carolina State Troops. My grandfather, Captain Hall commanded Company A—"The Irishmen" which were ordered to Camp Magnum, to become part of the new Second Regiment, to be commanded by Colonel William P. Blnum, commissioned on May 14, 1861. Upon the initial organization of the regiment in camp, and the completion of area recruitment of nearly 1,300 men to fulfill personnel requirements of 10 infantry companies and regimental headquarters field & staff; training of the regiment could begin in earnest. The Second was mustered into Confederate Service, and ordered to New Bern and transferred to the command of General French's Headquarters.

Upon the receipt of orders, the men and officers of the 2nd North Carolina State Troops were jubilant and full of anticipation of the battle glory's to come—when they would finally met the "dam Yankee" on the field of contest and honor, were transferred to Virginia! Later, the 7th North Carolina State Troops would follow the 2nd Regiment in organizing—they knew there patriotism and fidelity would lead to a triumph victory the regiment movement from Raleigh, North Carolina was timely and occurred without incident, arriving in New Bern for encampment. The regiment was detailed to coastal defensive and guard details in and around City of New Bern in front of the advancing federal army from the Atlantic coast.

During 1861 and early 1862, the war was well under way in Kentucky, Virginia, Missouri, Tennessee, and Louisiana. As of this time, the Confederacy had not as yet under taken any major campaign, the present emphasis was a war plan based on defensive posture—in other words waging a border war, buying time to muster available men and material from the interior states. The War and Naval Departments of the Confederacy needed time to develop war industries and procure all available arms and munitions from abroad. During this initial period they were aware that Gulf and Atlantic coastlines were relatively free of conquest, and the sea lanes were wide open for trade.

In mid-Summer, July 1862—the Forty-Sixth Regiment of North Carolina was finally relieved of inaction; coastal defense and guard duties, and ordered to proceed in all do haste to join the Army of Northern Virginia, headquartered at Richmond, under the command of General Robert E. Lee (a veteran Mexican War officer). (The war was changing gears to a more aggressive stance and a cry to take the battle to the enemy up North). The regiment had been assigned to Manning's Brigade, Walker's Division. The Left Wing (A.P. Hill's Corps). The Regimental Commander, Colonel Edward Dudley Hall, would be promoted to Brigadier-General and commanding Cooke's Brigade of North Carolina troops (i.e., 46th NC, 27th NC, and 48th NC), while the senior field officer; Lieutenant-Colonel William L. Saunders took command of the regiment.

Major Operation Fall of 1862: A contest for the Border States. The major Confederate strategy was a three prong invasion of Western Maryland—in hopes of the states' desire to secede. This was next to impossible, since the state was completely occupied by the federal forces.

The primary purpose of the invasion was secure enthusiastic recruits, and only secondly to check the federal army buildup-advance into the border state of Maryland and the defenses of its major support base in Baltimore on the tip of Chesapeake Bay. Two confederate corps proceeded north: General Jackson's Corp of the Shenandoah Valley from Winchester, Virginia through western Virginia, into western Maryland, objective: Harpers Ferry; General Longstreet's Corp of Central Virginia from Richmond, Virginia through central Maryland, objective: Sharpsburg, MD; and General Stuart's Cavalry Corps of Eastern Virginia making a Northeastern Virginia sweep through the lowlands, objective: Sharpsburg, MD. After a number of early successes, the central prong of the Confederate advance under General Lee was met by an over ambiguous federal army rush to Fredericksburg in December.

Lee's Army of Northern Virginia and the Forty-Sixth North Carolina would experience its first major combat action, on December 11, 1862 at the Battle of Fredericksburg near the town of like name. This would be a decisive victory for the Confederacy.

COL Charles W. L. Hall, PhD.
Confederate Historian

PART ONE
Hurrah for DIXIE . . . . !

THE
NORTH CAROLINA
DEFENSE

THE FORTY-SIXTH GOES TO CAMP . . .

CHAPTER I.

"Preparations for War"

The State Capitol: Raleigh, North Carolina 1861.

On May 20th, 1861 the North Carolina State Legislature voted to approve "secession" and declare the Great State of North Carolina a "sovereign nation!" The Adjutant-General's Office was given authority to raise and equip twelve North Carolina Regiments of Infantry from the counties of the state. To organize these twelve regiments into four infantry brigades, and commission four Brigadier-Generals to command these brigades in the defense of the state. A Major-General would be appointed by Governor Zebulon B. Vance, to oversee all State Troops, Reserves and Militia's, composing the military forces of North Carolina. The AG was further directed, to open Camp Mangum (just outside Raleigh), as a camp of instruction. Each regiment would be organized from locally recruited companies of volunteers, feed, sheltered, trained and armed from state stores and captured federal arsenals. Every one knew Lincoln was in the process of equipping a new federal army to invade the cotton states and quill the rebellion. A New Confederate Government had organized in February 22, 1861 in Montgomery, Alabama with the Honorable Jefferson Davis elected to serve as President and Commander-in-Chief. The stage was now set for all out warfare between the North and South. The Confederacy and the State of North Carolina did not have a minute to spare in making their preparations for WAR!

In March 1861, Brigadier-General Samuel G. French would be given the First North Carolina Infantry Brigade (7th N.C., 27th N.C., 35th N.C., Rogers Battalion, and Artillery) at New Bern.

PORT CITY: Wilmington, North Carolina 1861.

The lights of the city were burning day and night in excitement and overwhelming commerce of stores of all kinds. The merchant ships hardly spent any time at anchor, as there need to return to sea was enormous in profits. Speculation was wild throughout the local economy—all realizing the approaching storm of WAR. The local county sheriff, the honorable Edward Dudley Hall, was too aware of the silent but oncoming ferocious hurricane from the east. The New Hanover County Sheriff, had grown up on a Albemarle plantation, received his education at Donaldson Academy and entered state politics serving the legislature and now local county. He was an atypical southerner, fiercely patriot and a loyal aristocrat; he was soft spoken, intelligent and determined to keep his way of life for his children. He privately believed that the industrial

North would swoop down and destroy his home state. He felt he had no choice but to defend her to the end. So with his convictions, he sat about privately recruiting his own company of rough Irishmen. A hundred men or so were interested to volunteer and join Sheriff Hall's company. These big men wanted big guns—Hall's Company was designated as Heavy Artillery (hoping to find the big guns later) of New Hanover County, to be known as the "Rifle Rangers." 1

Heavy Artillery: Sheriff Hall resigned his office and enlisted as a private, when the unit was mustered in to state service by the AAG on April 16, 1861 at the state armory in Wilmington; Private Hall was elected Captain commanding on May 16th, 1861. Captain Hall received orders from Raleigh to take his men and man the artillery at old Fort Caswell, overlooking the sound—across from were the largest Confederate Fort every to be built, would be established (Fort Fisher). The Company would remain an unattached unit in State Troops until May 1861; the unit would see little or no action at this time. 1

"The Mighty 2nd North Carolina Infantry: The State AG ordered Captain Hall's Company to proceed by train north on the Wilmington & Weldon RR to Camp Advance, located at Graysburg, Northampton County for realignment and training. On June 2, 1861 this Heavy Artillery Company would be redesigned as Company "A" (also known as 1st Company A) and join the organizing 2nd North Carolina Infantry Regiment, State Troops. The regiment was ordered to Richmond, Virginia by train and arriving on July 19, 1861, proceeding to Camp Holmes in Stafford County."1

"On August 23, moved to Camp Potomac in King George County. The 1st N.C., 2d N.C., 3rd N.C., 1st Arkansas, and 30th Virginia now were banned together to form Walker's Brigade, command by Brigadier-General John G. Walker. In November 1861, the brigade entered winter quarters until January 14th, 1862. [As part of General Holmes's division] 6 the brigade was ordered south by rail to New Bern to defense against a new federal offensive there. Arriving March 25th at Camp Mac Intosh and under took general picket duty. (Captain Hall was transferred to Camp Mangum in late March 1862). There was little or no activity. In April 1862, the company would be detached and sent south on the W&W RR back through Wilmington, the old Fort Saint Philip, to again serve as Heavy Artillerymen." 1

FROM THE STATE CAPITOL TO THE ATLANTIC COAST . . .

CHAPTER II.

"The Defense of the Carolina Coast"

The Mighty 7th North Carolina Infantry: Captain Hall has been very effective and hardworking as a company commander, was selected by the AG for transfer to Camp Mason, near Graham, Alamance County to assist with organization of the 7th North Carolina Infantry Regiment, State Troops; and appointed Major on August 17th, 1861, of the field & staff. The 7th Infantry Regiment was ordered to deploy to Kinston and New Bern by way of the North Carolina RR and at Goldsboro, by way of the Atlantic & North Carolina RR, arriving in New Bern, and then marching 2 miles south of town to Fort Lane, on September 2, 1861. After securing the surrounding countryside, the 7th went into winter quarters at Fort Graham on December 4th; saw no action, breaking camp on March 5th, 1862. General Branch was in charge of New Bern defenses. The battle of New Bern was fought on March 14th, and lost to overwhelming federal forces. Major Hall was cited for personal bravery in leading a charge against theses forces. 1

The Mighty 46th North Carolina Infantry: The AG again selected Major Hall for reassignment based on his combat experience, and ordered him to Camp Mangum near Raleigh to rank as Colonel and command the newly commissioned 46th North Carolina Infantry Regiment, State Troops, on April 4th, 1862. 1

RURAL TOWN: Newton, North Carolina 1862.

In Randolph County, during the winter and spring of 1862 the war fever was running extremely high! The men of the surrounding county met in Newton, at the County Courthouse, and proposed the organization of a company under the leadership of a Mr. Obed Carr, to be known as the "Randolph Rangers!" In March 1862, a hundred volunteers sign up for three years service in the North Carolina State Troops. The men bead the families and kinsmen farewell and marched off for training at Camp Mangum near Raleigh, to prepare for WAR. This unit was mustered into state service by the AAG on April 4, 1862 as Company "G," and electing their leader to be Captain. 1

CAMP MANGUM (INSTRUCTION): Near Raleigh, 1862.

In order to mushroom the states military forces the state legislature authorized additional regiments, from April 21st to May 19th, 1862, the State Adjutant-General's Office would requisition, recruited and training nearly 15,000 men in fifteen regiments: 11th; 42d, 43d, 44th, 45th, 46th, 47th, 48th, 49th, 50th, 51st, 52d, 53d, 54th, and the 55th Infantry. 3

The 46th N.C. Infantry was being organized at Camp Mangum on April 4th (22d), 1862, under the able command of Colonel Edward D. Hall. The regiment was mustered into North Carolina State service on April 16th, 1862, "for three years or the duration of the war (whichever the shorter)." Later, transferred to Confederate service and placed under the direction of the War Department, CSA.

ONWARD TO RICHMOND: (and the baptism of fire!)

Completing training, the regiment was ordered to march to Goldsboro on May 6th, and board the train for Richmond, arriving on May 31st. June 2nd, the unit was immediately assigned for duty at Dewey's Bluff over looking the James River defenses, and took up station. While posted here, the 46th N.C., 27th N.C., 48th N.C., joined the 3d Ark., 30th Va. and the 2d Ga. Bn., in the brigade of Brigadier-General John G. Walker. 1

CENTRAL VIRGINIA and CITY OF RICHMOND, 1862

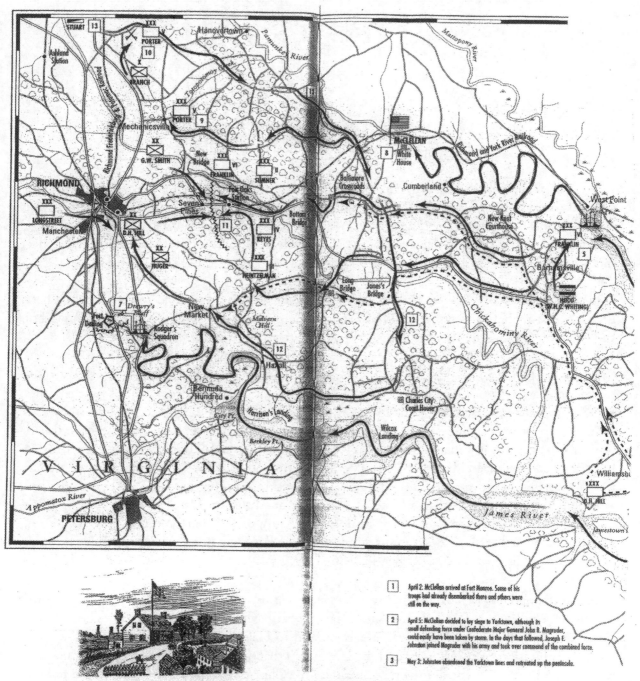

1 April 2: McClellan arrived at Fort Monroe. Some of his troops had already disembarked there and others were still on the way.

2 April 5: McClellan decided to lay siege to Yorktown, although its small defending force under Confederate Major General John B. Magruder, could easily have been taken by storm. In the days that followed, Joseph E. Johnston joined Magruder with his army and took over command of the combined force.

3 May 3: Johnston abandoned the Yorktown lines and retreated up the peninsula.

RE: THE ATLAS OF THE CIVIL WAR
M-2

THE FIRST DEFENSE OF RICHMOND CAPITOL AT MALVERN HILL . . .

CHAPTER III.

The first defense of Richmond Capitol
And the battle of Malvern Hill

July 1st, 1862: "Walker's Brigade remained at Dewey's Bluff until June 26th. On that date it was ordered to reinforce Major-General Benjamin Huger's division north of the James near King's School House, where the opening engagement of the Seven Days' campaign had occurred on June 25th. On June 27th the brigade was sent north of the Chickahominy River, where it remained until it was ordered back it was ordered back to rejoin Huger on the 29th." 1

"During the battle of Malvern Hill on July 1st, 1862 the brigade was subjected to heavy artillery fire from enemy batteries posted on Malvern Cliffs and from Federal gunboats on the James but suffered only light casualties. On July 2nd Walker's brigade returned to Dewey's Bluff." 1

"The brigade moved to Camp Lee, at Petersburg, Virginia, in mid-July and the various regiments were sent out on scouting and raiding missions to harass Federal ships on the James and Appomattox rivers. The brigade was ordered to Richmond on August 20th and went into camp just west of the city. On August 26th, it was sent by rail with Brigadier-General Robert Ransom's brigade to Rapidan Station, near Orange Courthouse. At about the same time the two brigades were organized into a division under the command of Walker (Walker was promoted to Major-General on November 8th, 1862). Colonel Van H. Manning of the 3rd Arkansas Infantry assumed temporary command of the Walker's former brigade. On September 1st, Walker's division moved from Rapidan Station to join the Army of Northern Virginia near Leesburg, where General Robert E. Lee was preparing to cross the Potomac River into Maryland. The army began fording the river on September 4th, 1862." 1

"Upon reaching Frederick, Maryland, two days later, the army halted, and General Lee dispatched Major-General Thomas J. Jackson to capture Harper's Ferry while Major-General James Longstreet's corps, of which Walker's division was a part, moved to Hagerstown. On September 9th, Walker moved his division from Monocracy Junction, near Frederick, to the month of the Monocracy River under instructions to destroy the aqueduct f the Chesapeake and Ohio Canal to prevent the enemy from escaping by that route. Across the river Major-General Lafayette McLaw's division, reinforced by Major-General Richard H. Anderson's division, occupied Maryland Heights while Jackson's troops occupied Bolivar Heights west of Harper's Ferry. Surrendered, the Federal garrison surrendered on September 15th, after a brief resistance." 1

MALVERN HILL, VIRGINIA 1862
(SEVEN DAYS BATTLES)

Union artillery at Malvern Hill, July 1 (above).
The expertly handled and directed Union batteries
proved far superior to those of the Confederacy, and
inflicted heavy casualties.

Malvern Hill
July 1, 1862

We have had one of the greatest
battles ever fought on this
continent and have driven the grand
army of the north from every position
they have taken. We have lost a great
many men but this must needs have
been."

A Georgia infantryman writing home, July 4.

RE: THE ATLAS OF THE CIVIL WAR

M-3

TABLE-1

ORDER OF BATTLE CONFEDERATE FORCES		
EASTERN VIRGINIA CAMPAIGN - THE SEVEN DAYS BATTLES		
JUNE 1862		
ARMY OF NORTHERN VIRGINIA, C.S.A.		
Commanding: General Robert E. Lee		
50,000 Men		
JACKSON'S COMMAND:		
	Commanding: Lt.Gen. Thomas J. Jackson	
WHITING'S DIVISION:		
	Comannding: Maj.Gen. Whiting	
		Hood's Brigade
		Law's Brigade
JACKSON'S DIVISION:		
	Commanding: Maj.Gen.	
		Winder's Brigade
		J.R. Jone's Brigade
		Fulkerson's Brigade
		Lawton's Brigade
EWELL'S DIVISION:		
	Commanding: Maj.Gen. Ewell	
		Elzey's Brigade
		Trimble's Brigade
		Seymour's Brigade
		Maryland Line Brigade
D.H. HILL DIVISION:		
	Commanding: Maj.Gen. D. H. Hill	
		Rodes'Brigade
		G.B. Anderson's Brigade
		Garland's Brigade
		Colquitt's Brigade
		Ripley's Brigade

LONGSTREET'S COMMAND:			
	Commanding: Lt.Gen. James Longstreet		
LONGSTREET'S DIVISION:			
	Commanding: Maj.Grn.		
		Kemper's Brigade	
		R.H. Anderson's Brigade	
		Pickett's Brigade	
		Wilcon's Brigade	
		Pryor's Brigade	
		Featherson's Brigade	
HUGHER'S DIVISION:			
	Commanding: Maj.Gen. Hugher		
		Mahone's Brigade	
		Wright's Brigade	
		Artistead's Brigade	
A. P. HILL'S DIVISION:			
	Commanding: Maj.Gen. A. P. Hill		
		Field's Brigade	
		Gregg's Brigade	
		J.R. Anderson's Brigade	
		Branch's Brigade	
		Archer's Brigade	
		Pender's Brigade	
HOLME'S DIVISION:			
	Commanding: Maj.Gen. Holmes		
		Ransom's Brigade	
		Daniel's Brigade	
		J.G. Walker's Brigade	
			27 N.C. Regt.
			46 N.C. Regt
			48 N.C. Regt.
			3 Ark Regt
			30 Va Regt
			2 Ga Bn
		Wise's Brigade	

MAGRUDER"S COMMAND:		
	Commanding: Maj.Gen. Magruder	
D. R. JONE"S DIVISION:		
	Commanding: Maj.Gen. D. R. Jones	
		Toomb's Brigade
		G.T. Anderson's Brigade
MC LAW"S DIVISION:		
	Commanding: Maj.Gen. Mc Law	
		Semmes' Brigade
		Kershaw's Brigade
MAGRUDER"S DIVISION:		
	Commanding: Maj.Gen.	
		Cobb's Brigade
		Griffith's Brigade
RESERVE ARTILLERY:		
	Commanding: Brig.Gen. Pendleton	
STUART"S CAVALRY COMMAND:		
	Commanding: Maj.Gen. J. E. B. Stuart	

THE CENTRAL MARYLAND CAMPAIGN AND THE BATTLE OF SHARPSBURG . . .

CHAPTER IV.

The Central Maryland Campaign (the battle of Sharpsburg).

September 17, 1862: "With the fall of Harper's Ferry, Lee ordered the army to concentrate at Sharpsburg, where the Federal army under General George B. McClellan was massing for an attack. When Walker's division arrived on the field on September 16th, it was positioned on the right flank of Lee's line. On the morning of September 17th the Confederate left, under Jackson, was vigorously assaulted, and Walker's division was ordered to reinforce Jackson."

"Colonel Edward D. Hall of the 46th Regiment, who assumed command of the brigade after Colonel Manning was wounded, reported the regiment's movements and activities after it went to the aid of Jackson as follows:

'I formed in line of battle . . . [my regiment being] on the left of the brigade. We advanced through a corn-field into a heavy raging furiously . . . Simultaneous with our entrance into the woods, the enemy commenced falling back in disorder . . . . On arriving at the far edge of the woods, I found the enemy in heavy force on an elevation, distance about 200 yards, with a battery of artillery in position on the crest of the hill. Between the enemy and the woods were two heavy panel fences, running obliquely. In face of such difficulties I thought it inexpedient to charge farther. I therefore placed my regiment behind a breastwork of rails, which I found, just beyond the woods, in short range of the enemy, and commenced firing . . . .

Being so far on the left, I had lost sight of the other regiments in the brigade, except the Thirtieth Virginia and a position of the Forty-eighth North Carolina, who, is attempting to charge over the fences and up the ascent, found themselves so massed up that they were compelled to lie down . . . . under a withering fire. In this position they suffered severely, and in a short time were compelled to retire.

. . . . .

The falling back of the Forty-eighth North Carolina and Thirtieth Virginia . . . left a wide gap open, which the enemy began at once to take advantage of in order to re-enter the woods, though [we kept up] a galling fire . . . on their advancing line until I deemed it unsafe . . . to remain in position while the enemy was massing upon [my] right and rear. The Forty-sixth, therefore, fell back . . . in good order . . . out of the woods . . . [I was then] met by General Jackson, who ordered me to report to General [Lafayette] McLaws. General McL[aws] ordered me to endeavor to hold the woods at all hazards. I then advanced in line of battle to the edge of the woods, which by that time was filled with the enemy, and placed the regiment behind a ledge of rocks, throwing out . . . skirmishers . . . A few minutes after, a brigade, which proved to be General [William] Barksdale's, passed on to my left. As soon as it entered the woods, I moved forward and came upon the right of General [Robert] Ransom's brigade, which . . . had succeeded in driving the enemy from the woods. Having only my own regiment with me, I informed General R(ansom] that I would connect myself with his command . . . We then took up our position in line of battle . . . and remained all day and night, the enemy evincing no desire to contest the woods with us, but satisfied himself with opening on us a very heavy fire of artillery . . . Although our losses by this fire considerable, we held the position until cessation of the battle. . . (Official Records, Series I, Volume XIX, part I, pages 918-919.)

General Ransom reported that the 46th [N.C.] Regiment "unflinchingly maintained" its position throughout the engagement and that its conduct was "all it should have been." (Official Records, Series I, Volume XIX, page 921.) Although severely crippled, the Confederate line held during the terrible day-long battle of September 17th. The next day the two armies rested on the field, and during the night of September 18th the Army of Northern Virginia retired across the Potomac and went into camp. During the Maryland campaign the 46th [N.C.] Regiment lost five men killed and sixty wounded.

The Army of Northern Virginia remained in the Shenandoah Valley until the Army of the Potomac began crossing the Blue Ridge Mountains on October 26th, 1862. On October 28th, Lee ordered Jackson's corps to move closer to Winchester, and Longstreet's corps, of which Walker's division was still a part, to move east of the mountains to Culpepper Courthouse." 1

In a different account of September 17th battle line: "A little before ten, General Walker, having been ordered from the right, pushed into the smoke and confusion of combat just behind Hood. Walker's division, consisting of Walker's own brigade and Ransom's brigade, was, with the exception of two regiments, composed of North Carolinians. His own brigade, under Manning and then under Col. E. D. Hall, of the Forty-sixth North Carolina, included the . . . the Forty-sixth, Colonel, and the . . . North Carolina regiments. As General Walker went in, he was notified that there was a gap of a third of a mile to the left of General Hill, and he detached the Twenty-seventh North Carolina and the Third Arkansas . . . to fill the gap, and well did they carry out their instructions. General McLaws' division from Harper's Ferry entered coincidently with Walker at 10:30 . . . Just then there were not enough Confederates in his front to stop a brigade, but Walker, as seen above, just arriving and McLaws was supporting him, and Early made a splendid use of his brigade. Walker at the head of his six North Carolina regiments and two others, "charging headlong," says Gen. J. D. Cox, who commanded the extreme Federal left . . . McLaw's, passing by Walker's left, also threw his division diagonally upon the already broken and retreating line [Federal line]." 4

"After Sharpsburg, the 46th Regiment N.C., [calling forth from the division commander especial mention of its gallant colonel {E. D. Hall} and staff for distinguished bravery and coolness under fire. During that day the {46th} regiment had occupied several positions of importance and great danger, and on every occasion it exhibited that steadiness and coolness which characterized its record]." 6

SHARPSBURG, MARYLAND 1862

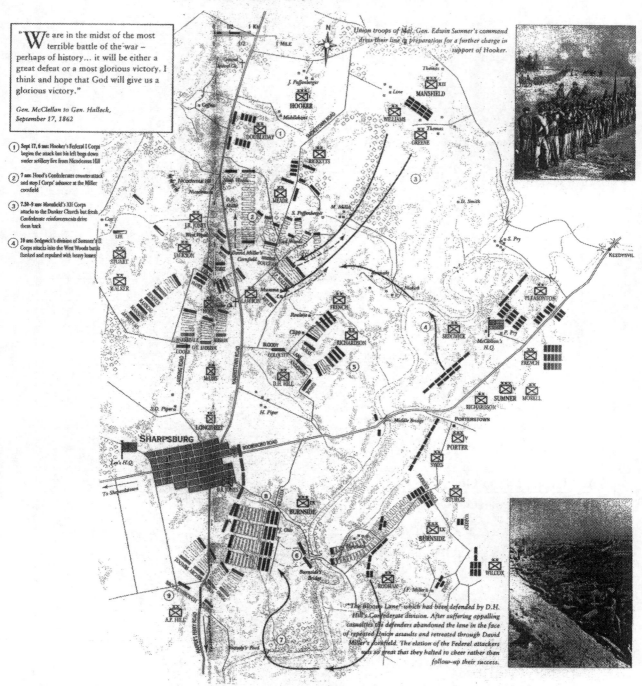

"We are in the midst of the most terrible battle of the war ~ perhaps of history... it will be either a great defeat or a most glorious victory. I think and hope that God will give us a glorious victory."

Gen. McClellan to Gen. Hallock, September 17, 1862

1 Sept 17, 6 am: Hooker's Federal I Corps begins the attack but his left bogs down under artillery fire from Nicodemus Hill

2 7 am: Hood's Confederates counterattack and stop I Corps' advance at the Miller cornfield

3 7.30–9 am: Mansfield's XII Corps attacks to the Dunker Church but fresh Confederate reinforcements drive them back

4 10 am: Sedgwick's division of Sumner's II Corps attacks into the West Woods but is flanked and repulsed with heavy losses

Union troops of Maj. Gen. Edwin Sumner's command dress their line in preparation for a further charge in support of Hooker.

"The 'Bloody Lane' which had been defended by D.H. Hill's Confederate division. After suffering appalling casualties the defenders abandoned the lane in the face of repeated Union assaults and retreated through David Miller's cornfield. The elation of the Federal attackers was so great that they halted to cheer rather than follow-up their success.

RE: THE ATLAS OF THE CIVIL WAR
M-4

TABLE-2

ORDER OF BATTLE CONFEDERATE FORCES		
MARYLAND MOUNTAIN CAMPAIGN - BATTLE OF SHARPSBURG		
SEPTEMBER 1862		
ARMY OF NORTHERN VIRGINIA, C.S.A.		
Commanding: General Robert E. Lee		
40,000 Men		
LEFT WING (2D CORPS) JACKSON'S:		
	Commanding: Lt.Gen. Thomas J. Jackson	
LAWTON'S DIVISION:		
	Comannding: Maj.Gen. Lawton	
		Douglas' Brigade
		Early's Brigade
		J.A. Walker's Brigade
		Hay's Brigade
J. R. JONE'S DIVISION:		
	Commanding: Maj.Gen. J. R. Jones	
		Grigsby's Brigade
		Warren's Brigade
		Johnson's Brigade
		Starke's Brigade
A. P. HILL'S DIVISION:		
	Commanding: Maj.Gen. A. P. Hill	
		Branch's Brigade
		Gregg's Brigade
		Brokenbrough's Brigade
		Archer's Brigade
		Pender's Brigade
		Thomas' Brigade
D.H. HILL DIVISION:		
	Commanding: Maj.Gen. D. H. Hill	
		Rodes' Brigade
		G.B. Anderson's Brigade

		Garland's Brigade	
		Colquitt's Brigade	
		Ripley's Brigade	

RIGHT WING (1ST CORPS) LONGSTREET'S:

| | Commanding: Lt.Gen. James Longstreet | | |
| | | | |

R. H. ANDERSON'S DIVISION:

	Commanding: Maj.Gen. R. H. Anderson		
		Cumming's Brigade	
		Posey's Brigade	
		Armistead's Brigade	
		Parham's Brigade	
		Pryor's Brigade	
		Wright's Brigade	

MC LAW'S DIVISION:

	Commanding: Maj.Gen.Mc Law		
		Kershaw's Brigade	
		Cobb's Brigade	
		Semmes' Brigade	
		Barksdale's Brigade	

D. R. JONE"S DIVISION:

	Commanding: Maj.Gen. D. R. Jones		
		Toomb's Brigade	
		Drayton's Brigade	
		Garrett's Brigade	
		Kemper's Brigade	
		J. Walker's Brigade	
		G.T. Anderson's Brigade	

J. G. WALKER"S DIVISION:

	Commanding: Maj.Gen. J. G. Walker		
		Manning's Brigade	
			27th N.C. Regt
			46th N.C. Regt
			48t N.C. Regt
			1st Ark Regt

			30th Va Regt
		Ransom's Brigade	

HOOD'S DIVISION:

	Commanding: Maj.Gen.John B. Hood		
		Wofford's Brigade	
		Law's Brigade	
		Evan's Brigade	

STUART"S CAVALRY COMMAND:

	Commanding: Maj.Gen. J. E. B. Stuart		
		Hampton's Brigade	
		Munford's Brigade	
		F. Lee's Brigade	

THE CENTRAL VIRGINIA CAMPAIGN
AND THE BATTLE OF FREDERICKSBURG ..

CHAPTER V.

The Central Virginia Campaign
And the battle of Fredericksburg

December 11th 1862: "When it began apparent that the Federal army, under its new commander, Major-General Ambrose E. Burnsides, was concentrating on the Rappahannock River across from Fredericksburg, General Lee ordered Longstreet's corps to take a position on the heights overlooking the town while Jackson's men went into a line Longstreet's right. During the movement General Walker was transferred, and General Ransom was placed in command of the division. Colonel John R. Cooke of the 27th Regiment N.C. Troops was promoted to brigadier-general and assigned to command Walker's (Manning's) former brigade. The 3d Regiment Arkansas Infantry and the 30th Regiment Virginia Infantry were transferred, and the 15th Regiment N.C. Troops (5th Regiment N.C. Volunteers) was assigned to the brigade on November 26th. Thus the 46th Regiment N.C. Troops, along with the 15th, 27th and 48th Regiments N.C. Troops, was part of Cooke's brigade of Ransom's division of Longstreet's corps." 1

"When Ransom's division arrived at Fredericksburg on November 19th, it was placed in a supporting position behind the artillery on Marye's Heights and Willis' Hill. During the Battle of Fredericksburg on December 13th, General Cooke was wounded, and Colonel Hall again assumed command of the brigade. Hall reported the brigade's part in the battle as follows:

'Early on the morning of the 11th instant the . . . .

Fredericksburg, where we remained in position until about 12 o'clock Saturday, the 13th, at which time the engagement was going on in our front. The brigade was formed in a line of battle as follows: The Twenty-seventh was on the right; Forth-eighth next; Forty-sixth next; Fifteenth on the left . . . . After advancing 200 yards under a heavy fire of shells and musketry, we arrived at the crest of Willis' Hill, which overlooks the battle-field, on which hill several batteries were placed. With the exception of the Twenty-seventh, the brigade was halted on the crest of the hill, and delivered its fire on the advancing column of the enemy, who was then engaged in making a furious assault on our frontal lines, which were covered by a long stone wall at the foot of the hill, which assault, on the arrival of the brigade, was repulsed, with great loss to the enemy. The enemy that time succeeded in getting up to 40 yards of the wall. After the repulse of the enemy, the Forty-sixth was moved down the hill behind the [wall], supporting [T.R.R.] Cobb's brigade, the Twenty-seventh and Forty-sixth remaining behind the [wall], and the Forty-eighth and Fifteenth on top of the hill all day. Six different times during he day did the enemy advance his heavily re-enforced columns, and each time was driven back with immense loss. The action ceased at night, when the brigade was withdrawal . . . . (Official Records, Series I, Volume XXI, pages 629-630.)'

"Quartermaster Sergeant John M. Waddill of the 46th Regiment reported the battle more succinctly:

'[On] 11 December the regiment . . . took position at the foot of the heights fronting the little city, and immediately behind the stone wall on Marye's Heights.

Here it awaited the attack by Burnside, and bore a full share in that historic slaughter. In comparative security, protected by the stone wall about breast high, all day long it shot down the brave men who charged again and again across the level plain in front, vainly yet most gallantly striving to accomplish impossibility. (Clark's Regiments, Volume III, pages 69-70.)'

During the Battle of Fredericksburg the 46th Regiment lost eleven men killed and fifty-seven wounded." 1

FREDERICKSBURG, VIRGINIA 1863

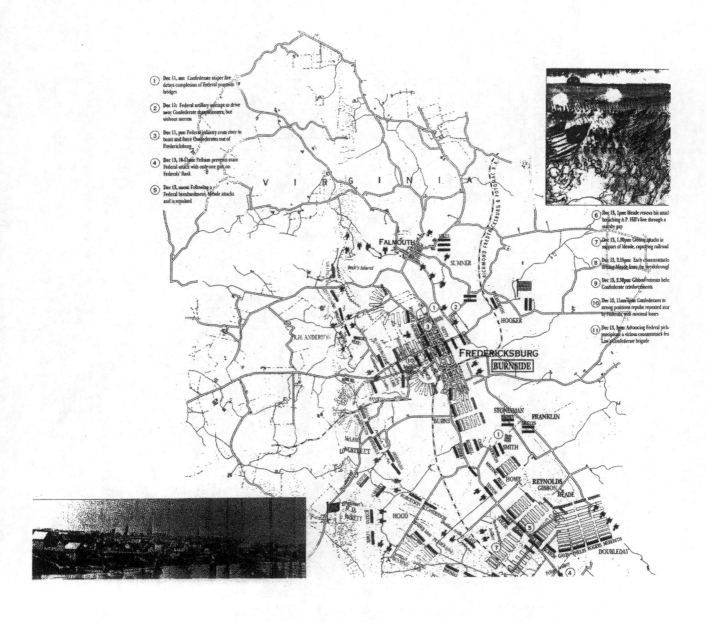

RE: THE ATLAS OF THE CIVIL WAR
M-5

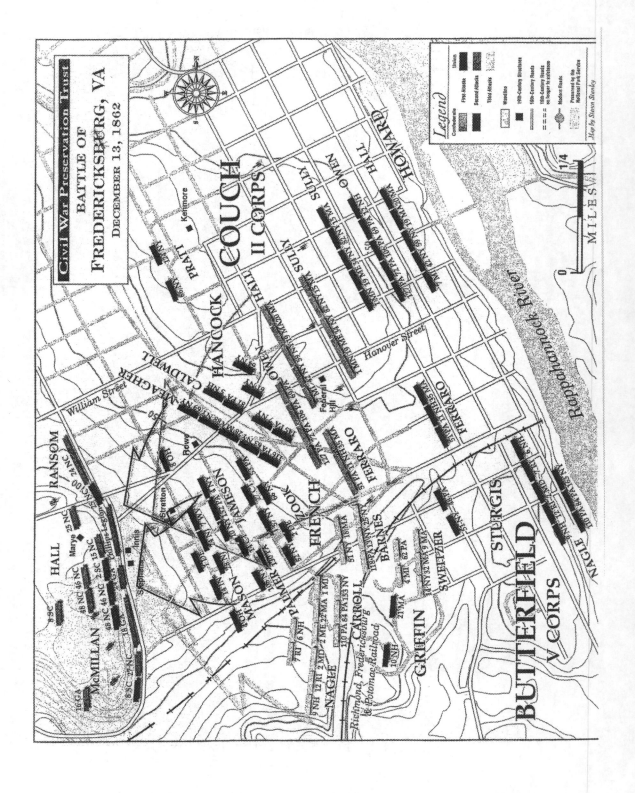

Civil War Preservation Trust
BATTLE OF
FREDERICKSBURG, VA
DECEMBER 13, 1862

TABLE-3

ORDER OF BATTLE CONFEDERATE FORCES		
NORTHERN VIRGINIA CAMPAIGN - BATTLE OF FREDERICKSBURG		
DECEMBER 1862		
ARMY OF NORTHERN VIRGINIA, C.S.A.		
Commanding: General Robert E. Lee		
78,000 Men		
2ND CORPS JACKSON'S:		
	Commanding: Lt.Gen. Thomas J. Jackson	
EARLY'S DIVISION:		
	Comannding: Maj.Gen. Jubal Early	
		Atkinson's Brigade
		Hoke's Brigade
		J.A. Walker's Brigade
		Hay's Brigade
TALIAFERRO'S DIVISION:		
	Commanding: Maj.Gen. Taliaferro	
		Paxton's Brigade
		Warren's Brigade
		Johnson's Brigade
		Pendelton's Brigade
A. P. HILL'S DIVISION:		
	Commanding: Maj.Gen. A. P. Hill	
		Lane's Brigade
		Gregg's Brigade
		Brokenbrough's Brigade
		Archer's Brigade
		Pender's Brigade
		Thomas' Brigade
D.H. HILL DIVISION:		
	Commanding: Maj.Gen. D. H. Hill	
		Rodes'Brigade
		Dole's Brigade

		Iverson's Brigade	
		Colquitt's Brigade	
		Grimes' Brigade	

1ST CORPS LONGSTREET'S:

	Commanding: Lt.Gen. James Longstreet		

R. H. ANDERSON'S DIVISION:

	Commanding: Maj.Gen. R. H. Anderson		
		Wilcox's Brigade	
		Featherson's Brigade	
		Mahone's Brigade	
		Perry's Brigade	
		Wright's Brigade	

MC LAW'S DIVISION:

	Commanding: Maj.Gen.Mc Law		
		Kershaw's Brigade	
		Cobb's Brigade	
		Semmes' Brigade	
		Barksdale's Brigade	

PICKETT"S DIVISION:

	Commanding: Maj.Gen.Pickett		
		Armistead's Brigade	
		Jenkin's Brigade	
		Garrett's Brigade	
		Kemper's Brigade	
		Corse's Brigade	

RANSOM"S DIVISION:

	Commanding: Maj.Gen.Ransom		
		Cooke's Brigade	
			27th N.C. Regt
			46th N.C. Regt
			48t N.C. Regt
			1st Ark Regt
			30th Va Regt
		Ransom's Brigade	

HOOD'S DIVISION:			
	Commanding: Maj.Gen.John B. Hood		
		G.T. Anderson's Brigade	
		Law's Brigade	
		Robertson's Brigae	
		Benning's Brigade	
STUART"S CAVALRY COMMAND:			
	Commanding: Maj.Gen. J. E. B. Stuart		
		Hampton's Brigade	
		W.H.F. Lee's Brigade	
		F. Lee's Brigade	
		W.E. Jones' Brigade	

The Mission to Poscataligo S.C. and the Battle at Bristoe Station . . .

CHAPTER VI.

The Mission to Pocotaligo Station, S.C. and the Battle of Bristoe Station.

January 3rd, 1863: "Cooke's brigade was ordered to South Carolina on January 3rd, 1863, and moved by stages to Petersburg, Goldsboro, and Wilmington, which it reached on or about February 18th. At a delay of several weeks in Wilmington and the vicinity, the regiment proceeded by rail to Charleston and then on to Coosawhatchie—about half way between Charleston and Savannah on the Charleston & Savannah Railroad. At Coosawhatchie the brigade was placed under the command of General P.G.T. Beauregard, commander of the Third Military District, Department of South Carolina, Georgia and Florida. The Forty-sixth Regiment was stationed about ten miles north of Coosawhatchie at Pocotaligo Station, which was promptly christened "The Devil's Misery Hole," for its "millions" of . . . . 70.) The other regiments of the brigade were detailed to support defensive positions along the railroad."

"On April 10th, 1863, the regiment, "with shouts of joy," left Pocotaligo Station for Charleston. (Clark's Regiments, Volume III, page 71.)"

"On or about April 22nd it entrained for Wilmington, where it arrived on April 26th. Several days later the brigade moved to Kinston to reinforce Major-General D.H. Hill's command, which had just failed in attempts to recapture New Bern and Washington, North Carolina. On May 22nd Cooke's brigade was sent to the support of the 56th Regiment N.C. Troops, which was being severely handled by a superior Federal force at Gum Swamp. After compelling the enemy to withdrawal, Cooke's brigade returned to Kinston. Shortly thereafter it was ordered to Richmond, where he 46th Regiment arrived on June 8th.

October 14th, 1863: "During the Gettysburg campaign in late June and early July, 1863, Cooke's brigade remained in the defenses around Richmond under the command of Major-General Arnold Elzey. The 46th Regiment was sent to Hanover Junction, about twenty-five miles north of Richmond, while the remainder of the brigade was stationed just north of the city on the Meadow Bridge Road. Two regiments (the 27th and 48th) were moved shortly thereafter to the South Anna Bridge on the Richmond & Fredericksburg Railroad, about fifteen miles north of Richmond.

When a Federal force advanced against that position, General Cooke was dispatched there with the 15ᵗʰ and 46ᵗʰ regiments on July 4ᵗʰ. After halting the Federals, Cooke's men remained on the South Anna until ordered to Fredericksburg when the Army of Northern Virginia returned to Virginia in mid-July after Gettysburg campaign. In early September the brigade was relieved and returned to Hanover Junction, where it remained until ordered to Gordonsville on or about September 27ᵗʰ. At Gordonsville it rejoined the Army of Northern Virginia and was assigned to Major-General Henry Heth's division of Lieutenant-General A.P. Hill's corps." 1

"When Cooke's brigade reported to Heth for duty on or about October 3ʳᵈ 1863, the Army of North Virginia was defending a line along the Rapidan River while the Army of the Potomac was in position on the Rappahannock River. When Lee heard that the Army of the Potomac had been weakened in order to send reinforcements to take part in Chattanooga campaign, he moved to strike the enemy's right flank. That maneuver compelled the Federal commander, General George G. Meade, to retire towards Centerville. As the rear guard of Meade's army passed through Bristoe Station on October 14ᵗʰ, Heth's division of Hill's corps came onto the field. Without warning for the rest of his command to come up or to reconnoiter, Hill ordered the attack, and the brigades of Cooke and Brigadier-General William W. Kirkland, unaware that they were heavily outnumbered and without support on their flanks, advanced down an open hill towards Federal troops entrenched behind a railroad embankment. Cooke's and Kirkland's brigades, swept by the murderous fire of three Federal divisions, were repulsed with heavy casualties. During the fighting General Cooke was wounded, [reportedly hit in the forehead while he was atop Willis's Hill] 5, 6 and Colonel Hall of the 46ᵗʰ Regiment again assumed command of the brigade. Colonel Hall reported the brigade's part in the battle as follows:

'After forming lines of battle . . . . Woods . . . the brigade was halted a few moments to correct the alignment. The enemy was discovered massed upon our left beyond the railroad and to the left of the road leading to this station. Being then in command of the extreme right regiment, I immediately discovered that the enemy was in heavy force on my right . . . In a few moments we were ordered to advance, and soon after the enemy's skirmishers began firing on my right flank. I discovered the line of battle behind the railroad, extending as far on my right as I could see; also a mass of troops lying perpendicular to the road . . . from which body an advance was made on my right in considerable numbers . . . . I sent my right company to engage the skirmishers . . . but they were soon driven in. I then changed the front of my regiment on the first company and checked their advance.

'The brigade again halted just before getting under fire, and I moved back just in time to join the line in its final advance . . . .

'Shortly afterwards information was brought me that General Cooke was wounded and that I was in command. I ordered my regiment to cease firing and passed up to the center of the brigade, stopping the firing as I went. The brigade was within 200 yards of the railroad. On getting on the top of the hill, I found the brigade suffering from a heavy flank fire of artillery from the right . . . . Also the guns on the left and rear of the railroad had an enfilading fire on us. The musketry fire from the line of [the] railroad was very heavy. I soon saw that a rapid advance must be made or a withdrawal. I chose the former. I passed the word to the [three] right regiments to charge . . . .

'The brigade charged up to within 40 yards of the railroad, and from the severity of the fire, and from seeing the extreme left on the line [composed of several companies of the Forty-eight to cross the Regiment] falling back, they [the brigade] fell back—the two right regiments [Forty-sixth and fifteenth] in good order, the third (Twenty-seventh North Carolina) in an honorable confusion, from the fact that between one-half to two-thirds of the regiment had been killed or wounded . . . . I halted the brigade in the first field we came to, about 400 yards from the enemy's line, from which positions we fell back beyond the second field on seeing the enemy come out on our right and left. After a short time the brigade of General [Joseph R.] Davis joined us on the right, when we again advanced to within 400 yards of the enemy . . . where we remained during the night. (Official Records, Series I, Volume XXIX, part 1, Pages 434-435.)

In the Chronicles of the Cape Fear River, James Sprunt, reports that the Bistoe Station was "An unequal struggle was waged, and disaster averted only by Colonel Hall's skillful management of his command." 6

"During the battle the regiment lost eight men killed and fifty-two wounded." 1

"No further attempts were made to attack the enemy at Bristoe Station, and during the night the Federal rear guard continued its retreat to Centerville. Lee retired to the Rappahannock and, after battles at Rappahannock Bridge and Kelly's Ford on November 7th, returned to the Rapidan. On November 26th, Meade began moving his army . . . . Men were strongly entrenched at Mine Run, and Meade unable to locate a vulnerable point against which to launch an attack, also began entrenching. On the morning of December 2nd, 1863 Lee sent an attack force of two divisions against what he believed to be an exposed Federal flank; however, when the Confederates moved forward they found that the Federal army had retreated. A pursuit was undertaken, but Meade recrossed the Rapidan unmolested. Lee ordered his troops into winter quarters, and the 46th Regiment spent the winter of 1863-1864 on picket duty along the rapidan and in camp with Cooke's brigade near Orange Courthouse." 1

In November 1863, Colonel Hall, having served as acting brigade commander of both Manning's and Cooke's brigades and having been cited for personal bravy and gallantry in several major engagements, was recommended for promotion to the rank of Brigadier-General. It was endorsed favorably by Generals Cooke, Heth, A.P. Hill and Lee, to the Secretary of War and then to President Davis; in turn a nomination was submitted for said promotion and signed off by the State Adjutant-General, Governor Vance, members of the State Legislature, and the N.C. Senators of the Confederate Congress. When both, the recommendation and the nomination reached the Confederate Executive Branch, the issue became involved in intense internal politics? His promotion now uncertain, Colonel Hall took a leave of absence and returned home to Wilmington to await the outcome of the debate.

Andrew Howell, in his book on Wilmington, gives a snapshot of the situation "President Jefferson Davis, of the Confederate States, visited Wilmington . . . . after delivering a public address on the November 4th 1863 . . . a regiment of soldiers were marched to Front and Princess Streets, where the President addressed them from the Princess Street entrance of the Bank of the State of North Carolina. The soldiers were under the command of Colonel E. D. Hall. The bands were playing the horses of the officers were prancing, and the whole scene was inspiring to lovers of the military display." 7

He refused to become involved in struggle and without a clear cut result; he tendered his resignation from the (Provisional) Confederate Army on December 27th, and with its acceptance on December 31st, 1863. On January 1st, 1864 returned to his role in the North Carolina Militia of New Hanover County, Wilmington as a Brigadier-General. Simulatiously, he was reelected and took civil office as County Sheriff.

Mr. Sprunt, states "the regiment lost its brilliant commander, a brave man, a good disciplinarian, a most valuable and efficient officer. It was with much regret that his regiment bade him farewell." 6, 3

BRISTOE STATION, VIRGINIA 1863

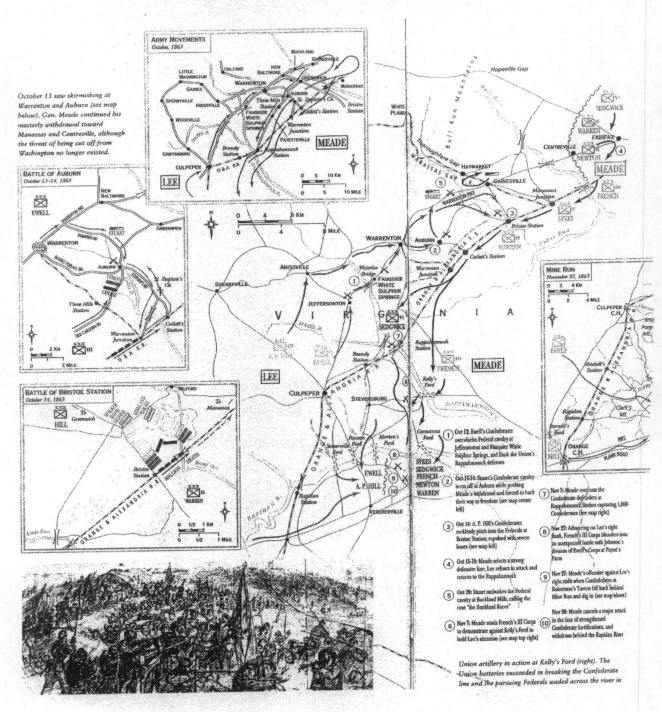

ARMY MOVEMENTS
October, 1863

October 13 saw skirmishing at Warrenton and Auburn (see map below). Gen. Meade continued his masterly withdrawal toward Manassas and Centreville, although the threat of being cut off from Washington no longer existed.

BATTLE OF AUBURN
October 13–14, 1863

BATTLE OF BRISTOE STATION
October 14, 1863

MINE RUN
November 27, 1863

① Oct 12: Ewell's Confederates overwhelm Federal cavalry at Jeffersonton and Fauquier White Sulphur Springs, and flank the Union's Rappahannock defenses.

② Oct 13–14: Stuart's Confederate cavalry is cut off at Auburn while probing Meade's withdrawal and forced to hack their way to freedom (see map left).

③ Oct 14: A. P. Hill's Confederates recklessly pitch into the Federals at Bristoe Station; repulsed with severe losses (see map left).

④ Oct 15–18: Meade selects a strong defensive line; Lee refuses to attack and returns to the Rappahannock.

⑤ Oct 20: Stuart ambushes the Federal cavalry at Buckland Mills, calling the rout "the Buckland Races".

⑥ Nov 7: Meade sends French's III Corps to demonstrate against Kelly's Ford to hold Lee's attention (see map top right).

⑦ Nov 7: Meade overruns the Confederate defenders x Rappahannock Station capturing 1,800 Confederates (see map right).

⑧ Nov 27: Advancing on Lee's right flank, French's III Corps blunders into an unexpected battle with Johnson's division of Ewell's Corps at Payne's Farm.

⑨ Nov 27: Meade's offensive against Lee's right stalls when Confederates fall back behind Mine Run and dig in (see map above).

⑩ Nov 30: Meade cancels a major attack in the face of strengthened Confederate fortifications, and withdraws behind the Rapidan River.

Union artillery in action at Kelly's Ford (right). The Union batteries succeeded in breaking the Confederate line and the pursuing Federals waded across the river in

RE: THE ATLAS OF THE CIVIL WAR
M-6

PART TWO

The Valorous Defense . . . . !!

THE
EASTERN
CAMPAIGN

THE BATTLE FOR THE WILDERNESS,

CHAPTER VII.

The Battle of the Wilderness.

May 4th 1864: "The brigade was still in camp near Orange Courthouse when the Federal army, under the strategic direction of General U.S. Grant, began crossing the lower Rapidan on the morning of May 4th, 1864, and entered an area of dense woods and tangled undergrowth known as the Wilderness. When news of Grant's crossing was received, Lee ordered Hill's corps to move towards the enemy by the Orange Plank Road and Lieutenant-General Richard S. Ewell's to advance on Hill's left down the Orange Turnpike. Lieutenant-General James Longstreet's corps, at Gordonville, was instructed to move up the Hill's right. On the morning of May 5th Hill's column clashed with Federal cavalry at Parker's Store and succeeded driving the enemy back. Hill's men then occupied the crossroads at Parker's Store. Immediately north of the Orange Turnpike. Ewell encountered the enemy in corps strength, and Hill ordered Heth's division to deploy across the Plank Road in anticipation of a Federal attack. Cooke's brigade was placed in the center of the Confederate line with Kirkland's brigade behind it in reserve. At 4:00 P.M., elements of the Federal II Corps attacked Heth's position and were repulsed with the aid of Kirkland's brigade after desperate fighting. After repelling several Federal assaults the Confederate counterattacked, but they were unable to dislodge the enemy. Severe fighting continued until Major-General Cadmus M. Wilcox's division arrived on the field and stabilized the Confederate line."

"Quartermaster Sergeant Waddill reported the day's slaughter as follows:

'A butchery pure and simple it was, unrelieved by any arts of war . . . . It was a mere slugging match in a dense thicket of small growth, where men but a few yards apart fired through the brushwood for hours . . . .

. . . .

All during the terrible afternoon, the Forty-sixth held its own, now gaining, now losing-resting at night on the ground over which it had fought, surrounded by the dead and wounded of both sides . . . . (Clark's Regiments, Volume III, pages 75-76.)

"During the night Cooke's battered brigade was withdrawn and placed in reserve to the left rear of Heth's position north of the Plank Road. Wilcox's division took up position south of the road."At 5:00 A.M. the next morning, May 6th, 1864, Federal columns struck the Confederate line in front and on the left flank. Thirteen Federal brigades fell upon Hill's eight brigades with such fury that there was no time for resistance, and the entire line fell back in disorder. Kirkland's men then rallied on Cooke's brigade, and other units joined in support of Cooke's position, but the Federals broke through again and a general rout followed. Only the timely arrival of Longstreet's corps, moving up to reinforce Hill, prevented the collapse of the right wing of Lee's army. The Federal assault was blunted and driven back, and Hill's men, after re-forming behind Longstreet, were dispatched to close a gap on the left of Longstreet's line. The battle continued on Longstreet's front until night brought an end to the fighting. During the Wilderness battle of May 5-6, 1864, the 46th Regiment, according to one unofficial report, lost thirty-five men killed and 251 wounded out of an effective strength of 540 men. (Clark's Regiments, Volume III, page 76.)" 1

THE BATTLE OF THE WILDERNESS, VIRGINIA 1864

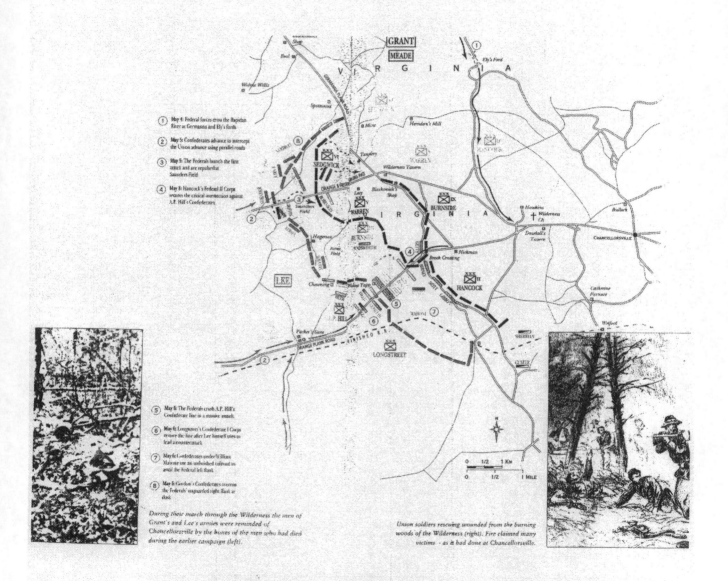

1 May 4: Federal forces cross the Rapidan River at Germanna and Ely's fords

2 May 5: Confederates advance to intercept the Union advance using parallel roads

3 May 5: The Federals launch the first attack and are repulsed at Saunders Field

4 May 5: Hancock's Federal II Corps secures the critical intersection against A.P. Hill's Confederates.

5 May 6: The Federals crush A.P. Hill's Confederate line in a massive attack.

6 May 6: Longstreet's Confederate I Corps restore the line after Lee himself tries to lead a counterattack.

7 May 6: Confederates under William Mahone use an unfinished railroad to assail the Federal left flank.

8 May 6: Gordon's Confederates overrun the Federals' unguarded right flank at dusk.

During their march through the Wilderness the men of Grant's and Lee's armies were reminded of Chancellorsville by the bones of the men who had died during the earlier campaign (left).

Union soldiers rescuing wounded from the burning woods of the Wilderness (right). Fire claimed many victims - as it had done at Chancellorsville.

RE: THE ATLAS OF THE CIVIL WAR
M-7

TABLE-4

ORDER OF BATTLE CONFEDERATE FORCES		
NORTHESTERN VIRGINIA CAMPAIGN - BATTLE OF THE WILDERNESS		
MAY 1864		
ARMY OF NORTHERN VIRGINIA, C.S.A.		
Commanding: General Robert E. Lee		
65,000 Men		
1ST CORPS:		
	Commanding: Lt.Gen. James Longstreet / R.H. Anderson	
KERSHAW'S DIVISION:		
	Comannding: Maj.Gen. Kershaw	
		Henagan's Brigade
		Humphrey's Brigade
		Wooford's Brigade
		Bryan's Brigade
FIELD'S DIVISION:		
	Commanding: Maj.Gen. Field	
		G.T. Anderson's Brigade
		Law's-Perry's Brigade
		Jenkin's-Bratton's Brigade
		Benning's-Du Bose's Brigade
2ND CORPS:		
	Commanding: Lt. Gen. Richard Ewell	
EARLY'S-GORDON'S DIVISION:		
	Commanding: Maj.Gen. Gordon	
		Hays'-Monaghan's Brigade
		Johnston's Brigade
		Pegram's-Hoffman's Brigade
		Gordon's-Evan's Brigade
JOHNSON'S DIVISION:		
	Commanding: Maj.Gen. Johnson	
		J.A. Walker's Brigade

		Stewart's Brigade
		Jones'-Witcher's Brigade
		Stafford's-York's Brigade

RODES' DIVISION:

	Commanding: Maj.Gen. Rodes	
		Daniel's Brigade
		Ramseur's Brigade
		Dole's Brigade
		Battle's Brigade

3RD CORPS HILL:

	Commanding: Lt.Gen. A. P. Hill / Jubal Early

R. H. ANDERSON'S DIVISION:

	Commanding: Maj.Gen. R. H. Anderson / Mahone	
		Perrin's Brigade
		Harris' Brigade
		Mahone's-Weisiger's Brigade
		Perry's Brigade
		Wright's Brigade

HETH"S DIVISION:

	Commanding: Maj.Gen. Henry Heth		
		Cooke's Brigade	
			27th N.C. Regt
			46th N.C. Regt
			48t N.C. Regt
			1st Ark Regt
			30th Va Regt
		Kirkland's Brigade	
		Davis' Brigade	
		H.H. Walker-Mayo's Brigade	

WILCOX'S DIVISION:

	Commanding: Maj.Gen. Wilcox	
		Lane's Brigade
		McGowan's Brigade
		Scales' Brigade
		Thomas' Brigade

STUART"S CAVALRY CORPS:		
	Commanding: Lt.Gen. J. E. B. Stuart	
HAMPTON'S DIVISION:		
	Commanding: Maj.Gen. Wade Hampton	
		Young's Brigade
		Rosser's Brigade
F. LEE'S DIVISION:		
	Commanding: Maj.Gen. Ftriz Lee	
		Lomax's Brigade
		Wickham's Brigade
W.H.F. LEE'S DIVISION:		
	Commanding: Maj.Gen. W.H.F. Lee	
		Chambliss' Brigade
		Gordon's Brigade

THE BATTLE FOR SPOTSYLVANIA

CHAPTER VIII.

The Battle of Spotsylvania

May 8th, 1864: "Late in the evening of May 7th it become apparent that Grant's army was on the march toward Spotsylvania Courthouse, throughout the night of May 7th Lee's men pushed southeastward in a race with the Federals to that strategic crossroads. The race was narrowly won by the Confederates on the morning of May 8th, and a strong defensive line was quickly constructed. Hill's corps, under temporary command of Major-General Jubal A. Early, was positioned on the right of the line with Ewell's corps in the center and Longstreet's corps, under temporary command of Major-General Richard H. Anderson, on the left. Heth's division occupied the extreme right of the Confederate line until May 10th, when it was moved to the extreme left of the line to attack an exposed Federal flank. After inconclusive fighting with the Federal reconnaissance force at Wait's Shop, Heth's men returned to their original position on the Confederate right on the morning of May 11th." [1]

"Early on the morning of May 12th the Federals launched a sudden attack against a convex, U-shaped salient in the center of the Confederate line known as the "Mule Shoe," overran the salient at its apex, and began driving the survivors back. After vicious hand-to-hand fighting. Confederate reinforcements managed to check the Federal assault while a new line was constructed across the base of the salient. Cooke's brigade was not involved in the Mule Shoe battle but did extend its front in order to cover the area vacated by the reinforcements sent to stem the Federal attack" [1]

SPOTSYLANIA, VIRGINIA 1864

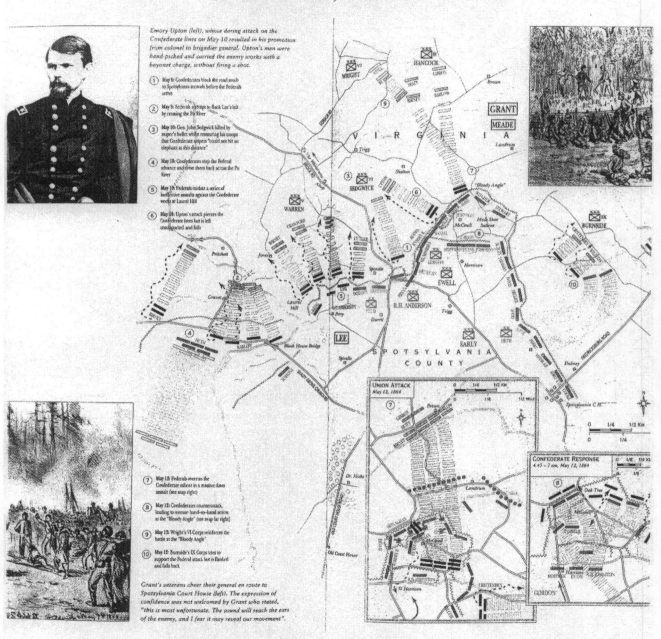

Emory Upton (left), whose daring attack on the Confederate lines on May 10 resulted in his promotion from colonel to brigadier general. Upton's men were hand-picked and carried the enemy works with a bayonet charge, without firing a shot.

1. May 8: Confederates block the road south to Spotsylvania seconds before the Federals arrive

2. May 9: Federals attempt to flank Lee's left by crossing the Po River

3. May 10: Gen. John Sedgwick killed by sniper's bullet while reassuring his troops that Confederate snipers "could not hit an elephant at this distance"

4. May 10: Confederates stop the Federal advance and drive them back across the Po River

5. May 10: Federals initiate a series of ineffective assaults against the Confederate works at Laurel Hill

6. May 10: Upton's attack pierces the Confederate lines but is left unsupported and fails

7. May 12: Federals overrun the Confederate salient in a massive dawn assault (see map right)

8. May 12: Confederates counterattack, leading to intense hand-to-hand action at the "Bloody Angle" (see map far right)

9. May 12: Wright's VI Corps reinforces the battle at the "Bloody Angle"

10. May 12: Burnside's IX Corps tries to support the Federal attack but is flanked and falls back

Grant's veterans cheer their general en route to Spotsylvania Court House (left). The expression of confidence was not welcomed by Grant who stated, "this is most unfortunate. The sound will reach the ears of the enemy, and I fear it may reveal our movement".

UNION ATTACK
May 12, 1864

CONFEDERATE RESPONSE
4:45 – 7 am, May 12, 1864

RE: THE ATLAS OF THE CIVIL WAR
M-8

THE BATTLE OF COLD HARBOR . . .

CHAPTER IX.

The Battle of Cold Harbor.

June 3rd 1864: "Following several more unsuccessful attempts against the Confederate line during the next week, Grant began moving eastward. Lee then moved his army to the North Anna River to a point just north of Hanover Junction, where he blocked the Federal route of advance. Several days of inconclusive fighting, in which Heth's division was not directly involved, convinced Grant of the tactical inferiority of his position on the North Anna, and on the night of May 26th he recrossed the river and moved eastward toward the Pamunkey." 1

"Lee began shifting his army southward as soon as it was learned that Grant was again on the move, and on May 27th Ewell's corps, temporarily commanded by General Early (General Hill had returned to command his own corps on May 21st), marched some twenty-four miles and entrenched between Beaver Dam Creek and Pole Green Church. Longstreet's corps, still under the command of Anderson, came up on Early's right, and Hill's corps extended the line on Early's left. On May 30, under orders from Lee, Early attacked the Federal left at Bethesda Church. The attacks received a sharp rebuff but did discover that the enemy was again siding to the Confederate right." 1

"The two armies began concentrating at Cold Harbor, where new fighting broke out on June 1st. The next day two of Hill's divisions, commanded by Major-General Cadmus M. Wilcox and Brigadier-General William Mahone, were ordered to leave their positions on the left of the Confederate line and to go to the support of Anderson, on the right. While Wilcox and Mahone moved to anchor the Confederate right, Heth's division, still in its original position on the left, joined Ewell's (Early's) corps in an attack which, after some initial success, was beaten off by Federal reinforcements." 1

"At 4:30 A.M. on June 3 the Federal launched a frontal attack against the six-mile-long Confederate line. Three separate assaults against Heth's well-entrenched division were repulsed, and at other points along the line the Federal attackers were driven back with appalling casualties. At about 11:00 A.M. the Federal assaults ceased, but infantry and artillery fire continued from defensive positions until 1:00 P.M. Heth's division was ordered to the right to rejoin Hill's corps at Turkey Hill in late afternoon." 1

THE BATTLE OF COLD HARBOR, VIRGINIA 1864

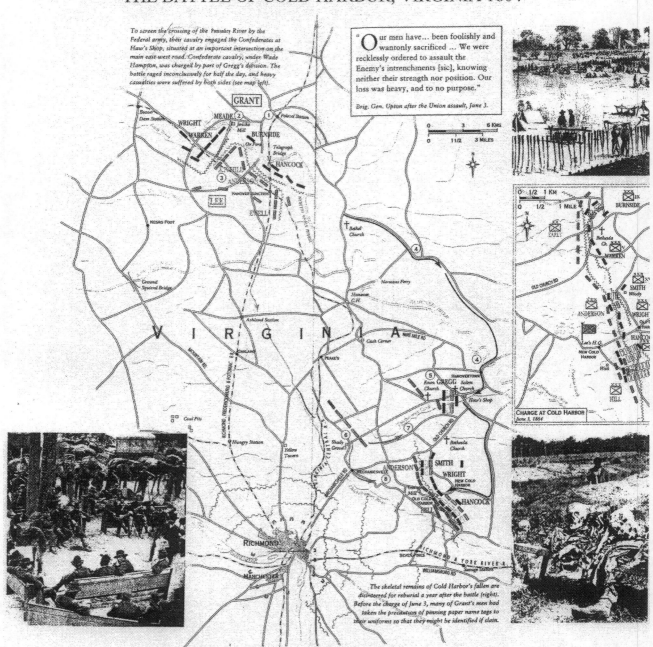

To screen the crossing of the Pamunkey River by the Federal army, their cavalry engaged the Confederates at Haw's Shop, situated at an important intersection on the main east-west road. Confederate cavalry, under Wade Hampton, was charged by part of Gregg's division. The battle raged inconclusively for half the day, and heavy casualties were suffered by both sides (see map left).

"Our men have... been foolishly and wantonly sacrificed ... We were recklessly ordered to assault the Enemy's intrenchments [sic], knowing neither their strength nor position. Our loss was heavy, and to no purpose."

Brig. Gen. Upton after the Union assault, June 3.

CHARGE AT COLD HARBOR
June 3, 1864

The skeletal remains of Cold Harbor's fallen are disinterred for reburial a year after the battle (right). Before the charge of June 3, many of Grant's men had taken the precaution of pinning paper name tags to their uniforms so that they might be identified if slain.

RE: THE ATLAS OF THE CIVIL WAR
M-9

PART THREE

The Twilights last gleaming . . .

THE
WESTERN
RETREAT

THE ALL-HAZARDS DEFENSE AND FINAL BATTLE LINE AT THE RICHMOND CAPITOL . . .

CHAPTER X.

**The All-hazards defense and
final battle line at the Richmond Capitol.**

May 5th, 1864 ?: "The two armies settled into defensive positions, where they remained until Grant began marching south towards the James River on June 12th. Lee followed on June 13th and made contact with the enemy at Rid dell's Shop the same day. On June 15 the 46th Regiment lost about twenty-five men in a small battle at White Oak Swamp. Grant then crossed the James and moved against Petersburg. Hill's corps at arrived Petersburg on June 18th and went into position on the extreme right of the line, which, which was thereby extended to the Petersburg & Weldon Railroad. Heth's division began entrenching and remained in line until July 28th, when in was ordered to the north side of the James to confront a Federal advance that was later revealed to be a Federal feint. Heth's division returned to Petersburg on August 2nd after the withdrawal of the Federal feint and the failure of Grant's Petersburg mine assault on July 30th. Heth's men then enjoyed three weeks of relative quiet." 1

TABLE-5

ORDER OF BATTLE CONFEDERATE FORCES		
FINAL BATTLE LINE - THE RICHMOND CAPITOL		
JUNE 15, 1864		
ARMY OF NORTHERN VIRGINIA - C.S.A.		
Commander: General Robert E. Lee		
50,000 Men		
ARMY SUPPORT ELEMENTS:		
	Provost Guard Commander: Maj. D.B. Bridgeford	
		1st Va Bn
		39th Va Bn Cav

		Army Engineers Commander: Col. T.M.R. Talcott
		1st Confederate Engineers
		2nd Confederate Engineers
FIRST ARMY CORPS:		
	Commanding: Maj.Gen. Richard H. Anderson	
PICKETT'S DIVISION:		
	Commanding: Maj.Gen. George E. Pickett	
		STEUARTS'S BRIGADE:
		(5 Virginia Regts.)
		CORSE'S BRIGADE:
		(5 Virginia Regts.)
		HUNTON"S BRIGADE:
		(5 Virginia Regts.)
		TERRY"S BRIGADE:
		(5 Virginia Regts.)
FIELD"S DIVISION:		
	Commanding: Maj.Gen. Charles W. Field	
		BRATTON"S BRIGADE:
		(4 S.C. Regts, 1 SS Bn)
		ANDERSON"S BRIGADE:
		(5 Georgia Regts)
		LAW"S BRIGADE:(Perry)
		(5 Alabama Regts)
		GREGG"S BRIGADE:
		(3 Tx, 1 Ark Regt)
		BENNING"S BRIGADE: (DuBose)
		(4 Georgia Regts)
KERSHAW"S DIVISION:		
	Commanding: Brig.Gen. Joseph B. Kershaw	
		KERSHAW'S BRIGADE: (Henagan)
		(5 S.C. Regts, 1 Bn.)
		HUMPHREY"S BRIGADE:
		(4 Mississippi Regts)
		WOFFORD"S BRIGADE:
		(3 Ga Regts, 2 Legions)
		BRYAN"S BRIGADE: (Simms)
		(4 Georgia Regts)

THIRD ARMY CORPS:			
	Commanding: Lt.Gen. A. P. Hill		
CORPS SUPPORT ELEMENTS:			
			5TH Alabama Bn.
ANDERSON'S DIVISION:			
	Commanding: Brig.Gen. William Mahone		
		SANDER"S BRIGADE:	
			(5 Alabama Regts)
		MAHONE"S BRIGADE: (Weisiger)	
			(5 Virginia Regts)
		HARRIS"S BRIGADE:	
			(4 Mississippi Regts)
		WRIGHT"S BRIGADE:	
			(3 Ga Regts, 2 Ga Bn.)
		PERRY"S BRIGADE: (Finagan)	
			(6 Florida Regts)
HETH"S DIVISION:			
	Commanding: Maj.Gen. Henry Heth		
		DAVIS" BRIGADE:	
			(4 Miss Regts, 1 N.C. Regt)
		COOKE"S BRIGADE:	
			15th N.C. Regt
			27th N.C. Regt
			46th N.C. Regt
			48th N.C. Regt
		KIRKLAND"S BRIGADE: (MacRae)	
			(5 N.C. Regts)
		FRY"S BRIGADE: (Mayo)	
			(1 Ala, 2 Tn, 3 Va, 2 Bn-Md, Va)
WILCOX'S DIVISION:			
	Commanding: Maj.Gen. Cadmus M. Wilcox		
		THOMAS" BRIGADE:	
			(4 Georgia Regts)
		LANE'S BRIGADE:	
			(5 N.C. Regts)

		MC GOWAN"S BRIGADE:
		(4 S.C. Regts)
		SCALES" BRIGADE:
		(5 N.C. Regts)

CAVALARY CORPS:

	Commanding: Maj.Gen. Wade Hampton	
		DUNOVANT"S BRIGADE:
		(4 S.C. Regts)
		YOUNG"S BRIGADE:
		(1 Ga Regt, 3 Legions, 2 Bn)
		ROSSER"S BRIGADE:
		(3 Va Regts, 1 Bn)

FITZHUGH LEE"S DIVISION:

	Commanding: Maj.Gen. Fitzhugh Lee	
		WICKHAM"S BRIGADE:
		(4 Virginia Regts)
		LOMAX"S BRIGADE:
		(3 Virginia Regts)

W.H.F. LEE"S DIVISION:

	Commanding: Maj.Gen. W.H.F. Lee	
		BARRINGER"S BRIGADE:
		(4 N.C. Regts)
		CHAMBLISS" BRIGADE:
		(3 Virginia Regts)

ARMY ARTILLERY:

	Commanding: Brig.Gen. William N. Pendleton

FIRST CORPS ARTILLERY:

	Commanding: Brig.Gen. E.Porter Alexander

SECOND CORPS ARTILLERY:

	Commanding: Brig.Gen. Armistead L. Long

THIRD CORPS ARTILLERY:

	Commanding: Col. R. Lindsay Walker

HORSE ARTILLERY:

	Commanding: Maj. R. Preston Chew

DEPARTMENT N.C. & SOUTHERN VIRGINIA - C.S.A.

	Commanding: General P.G.T. Beauregard

JOHNSON"S DIVISION:		
	Commanding: Maj.Gen. Bushrod R. Johnson	
		ELLIOT"S BRIGADE:
		(5 S.C. Regts)
		GRACIE"S BRIGADE:
		(3 Ala Regs, 1 Bn)
		JOHNSON"S BRIGADE: (Fulton)
		(5 Tennessee Regts)
		DIVISION ARTILLERY:
		(2 Bn)
HOKE"S DIVISION:		
	Commanding: Maj.Gen. Robert F. Hoke	
		CLINGMAN"S BRIGADE:
		(4 N.C. Regts)
		COLQUITT"S BRIGADE:
		(5 Georgia Regts)
		HAGOOD"S BRIGADE:
		(4 S.C. Regts, 1 Bn)
		MARTIN"S BRIGADE:
		(4 N.C. Regts)
		DIVISION ARTILLERY:
		(1 Bn)
DEPARTMENT OF RICHMOND - C.S.A.		
	Commanding: Lt.Gen. Richard S. Ewell	
		RANSOM"S BRIGADE:
		(5 N.C. Regts)
		CAVALRY BRIGADE: (Martin)
		(1 S.C., Va, 1 Legion)
		LOCAL DEF TRPS/RES BRIGADE:
		(1 Res Regt, 6 Bn)
	Unassigned:	
		(1 Ala Regt, 3 Bn)
		ARTILLEY DEFENSE UNITS:
		(8 Bn)

THE BATTLE LINE FOR RICHMOND, 1864

The Drewry's Bluff Campaign MAY 5–16 1864

As part of General Grant's master plan for the defeat of the Confederacy in 1864, General Butler was to lead a small Federal army up the James River toward the southern approaches of Richmond. If all went well, Butler would meet Grant near the Confederate capital within ten days of the opening of the campaign. Styled the Army of the James, Butler's force numbered approximately 40,000 troops. On May 5, convoyed by the navy, Butler sailed up the James and landed at Bermuda Hundred, less than 20 miles from Richmond. Although initially he encountered no significant opposition, Butler spent several days establishing a defensive enclave before attempting major offensive operations.

Because all Confederate units available to reinforce the Virginia theater were under orders to join the Army of Northern Virginia, the south side of the James was defended by only a few troops under General Beauregard. Caught off guard by the Federal landing, which was nearer Richmond than most of his own troops, Beauregard hastily began to concentrate a strike force from the Carolinas by rail. For several days, however, he could do nothing but view Butler's activities with alarm. Fortunately for the Confederates, Butler did little more than lightly damage the Richmond & Petersburg Railroad before he finally began an advance toward Richmond on May 12.

The week Butler spent at Bermuda Hundred permitted him to perfect a fortified base at Bermuda Hundred the City Point, but it also permitted Beauregard to gather an almost

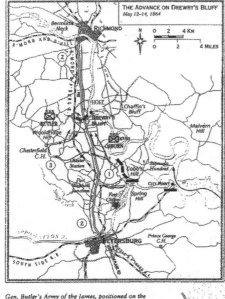

The Advance on Drewry's Bluff, May 12–14, 1864

① The Army of the James digs defensive lines (see map left)

② May 11: Having collected reinforcements, Beauregard marches north, meeting troops heading south from Richmond

③ May 12: Butler advances toward Richmond (see map left)

④ May 16: Confederates advance out of early morning mist and clash with Union right

⑤ Hoke advances against Gilmore's Union divisions. Heavy losses incurred by both sides in confused engagements exacerbated by fog

⑥ Beauregard orders Colquit forward into gap between Ransom and Hoke's Confederate divisions

⑦ After pressing forward most of the day suffering 2500 casualties and not receiving cavalry assistance expected from the south west, Beauregard orders army into night positions

⑧ Butler withdraws during the night to Bermuda Hundred

Gen. Butler's Army of the James, positioned on the Peninsula, was to take part in Gen. Grant's master plan to crush the Confederate armies and end the war before November. On May 5, after steaming up the James River, Butler's forces landed midway between Petersburg and Richmond. Instead of moving quickly to cut the railroad between the two cities, and entering Richmond against the opposition, Butler first dug defensive lines then, after a week's delay, began a cautious advance on the Confederate capital. By then, however, Gen. Beauregard's meagre forces had been reinforced, and he was able to meet the Federals at Drewry's Bluff on almost equal terms (see map above).

Although he had supported the State's Rights candidate against Lincoln in 1860, Benjamin Butler (below) quickly raised a volunteer regiment for the Union after Fort Sumter fell. An astute politician and lawyer, Butler was a failure in the military and eventually resigned his commission in November 1865.

equivalent force at Petersburg. Marching northward across Butler's front on May 11, Beauregard joined troops from the Department of Richmond and barred Butler's route to the Confederate capital. By May 15, the Army of the James had gained an outer Confederate defense line, but was unable to advance further. Seizing the initiative, Beauregard on May 16 struck Butler's army a devastating blow in the battle of Drewry's Bluff, and drove it within its Bermuda Hundred entrenchments. This action alone cost 3,004 Federal casualties and 2,966 Confederate. Although Butler and Beauregard retained some freedom of movement, the approach of the main armies soon siphoned troops from the Bermuda Hundred front, which subsided into stalemate for the remainder of the war.

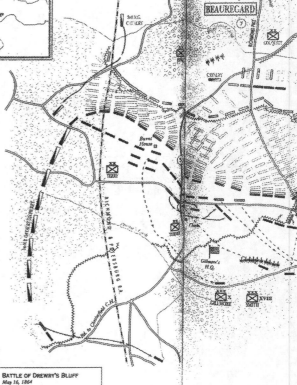

Battle of Drewry's Bluff, May 16, 1864

RE: THE ATLAS OF THE CIVIL WAR
M-10

THE ATTEMPTED TRENCH DEFENSE AND FINAL BATTLE LINE OF PETERSBURG . . .

CHAPTER XI.

**The Attempted Trench defense and
Final battle line of Petersburg.**

August 25th, 1864: "In mid-August, 1864, General Grant ordered an extension of his line to the west, and on August 18th a Federal force occupied Globe Tavern on the Petersburg & Weldon Railroad. Hill's corps was engaged at Globe Tavern on August 18-21 in an unsuccessful effort to dislodge the Federals. South of Globe Tavern a Federal force that had occupied Reams' Station and was destroying the railroad south of that point was attacked by Hill on August 25th. An assault by two brigades was repulsed, but a stronger attack on the Federal right in which Cooke's brigade took part succeeded in breaking the Federal line. Some 2,000 men and nine pieces of artillery were captured, and the Federals were driven from the field in disorder. Hill's corps returned to the Petersburg trenches that night." 1

"Heth's division did see action again until September 30th when the Confederates, in an unsuccessful attempt to prevent Grant from extending his line westward from Globe Tavern, were defeated at Jones' Farm. On October 27th a Federal force attempted to cut the Boydton Plank Road and Southside railroad by gaining possession of the high ground north of Hatcher's Run at Burgess' Mill. Hill concentrated Heth's and Mahone's divisions and Major-General Wade Hampton's cavalry force to oppose that advance and, while Heth's men held the Confederate center, sent Mahone against the Federal right and Hampton against the left. Mahone's attack failed, but the simultaneous attack on the left achieved a measure of success and was pressed vigorously until dark. The Federals withdrew the next day, and Cooke's brigade marched to a camp near Hatcher's Run and went into winter quarters." 1

"On December 8th Cooke's brigade, with the remainder of Hill's corps, was ordered to Belfield to oppose a Federal advance on the Petersburg & Weldon Railroad. Marching through sleet and snow, the Confederates arrived at a point a few miles from Belfield where they learned that the Federals had retired. Hill then attempted to cut off the enemy's retreat and intercepted the Federal cavalry at Jarratt's Station. After a brief skirmish the Confederates pushed on, but the Federal infantry was three hours ahead of them and could not be overtaken. Hill then called off the pursuit and bivouacked for the night; his men then returned to Hatcher's Run. Except for picket skirmishers, Cooke's brigade was in no further action for the remainder of the year." 1

"Early in February 1865, General Grant ordered a move on the left of his line to interdict Confederate supply-wagon traffic on the Boydton Plank Road at Hatcher's Run. Cooke's brigade led an n assault on the new Federal position on February 5th, but finding themselves inadequately supported by a brigade on the left flank that failed to assume its assigned position, Cooke's men fell back in the face of mounting Federal pressure. After more skirmishing on February 6th, the brigade returned to its former camp." 1

"Following almost two months of relative quiet, during which they were subjected to sporadic sniping and artillery fire, Cooke's men marched to Petersburg on the night of March 24th and formed in line to take part in an attack on Fort Stedman, a key Federal fortification whose capture would endanger Grant's line of supply and help relieve the intensifying pressure on the Richmond-Petersburg defenses. Cooke's brigade was held in reserve during the Confederate assault, which, after some initial success, was shattered by a massive Federal counterattack. The brigade then returned to its camp." 1

TABLE-6

ORDER OF BATTLE CONFEDERATE FORCES			
FINAL BATTLE LINE - PETERSBURG DEFENSES			
MARCH 1,1865			
ARMY OF NORTHERN VIRGINIA - C.S.A.			
Commander: General Robert E. Lee			
25,000 Men			
ARMY SUPPORT ELEMENTS:			
	Provost Guard Commander: Maj. D.B. Bridgeford		
		1st Va Bn	
		44th Va Bn Co B	
	Escort:		
		39th Va Bn Cav	
	Army Engineers Commander: Col. T.M.R. Talcott		
		1st Confederate Engineers	
		2nd Confederate Engineers	
FIRST ARMY CORPS:			
	Commanding: Lt.Gen. James Longstreet		
PICKETT'S DIVISION:			
	Commanding: Maj.Gen. George E. Pickett		
		STEUARTS'S BRIGADE:	
			(5 Virginia Regts.)
		CORSE'S BRIGADE:	
			(5 Virginia Regts.)
		HUNTON"S BRIGADE:	
			(5 Virginia Regts.)
		TERRY"S BRIGADE:	
			(5 Virginia Regts.)
FIELD"S DIVISION:			
	Commanding: Maj.Gen. Charles W. Field		
		BRATTON"S BRIGADE:	
			(4 S.C. Regts, 1 SS Bn)
		ANDERSON"S BRIGADE:	
			(5 Georgia Regts)

		LAW"S BRIGADE:(Perry)
		(5 Alabama Regts)
		GREGG"S BRIGADE:
		(3 Tx, 1 Ark Regt)
		BENNING"S BRIGADE: (DuBose)
		(4 Georgia Regts)

KERSHAW"S DIVISION:

Commanding: Brig.Gen. Joseph B. Kershaw

		DUBOSE"S BRIGADE:
		(3 Georgia Regts, 1 SS Bn)
		HUMPHREY"S BRIGADE:
		(4 Mississippi Regts)
		SIMMS" BRIGADE:
		(4 Georgia Regts)

SECOND ARMY CORPS:

	Commanding: Lt.Gen. John R. Gordon

GRIMES" DIVISION:

	Commanding: Maj.Gen. Bryan Grimes

		BATTLES" BRIGADE: (Hobson)
		(5 Alabama Regts)
		GRIME"S BRIGADE: (Coward)
		(4 N.C. Regts, 1 Bn)
		COX"S BRIGADE:
		(6 N.C. Regts)
		COOK"S BRIGADE: (Nash)
		(4 Ga Regts, 1 Bn)

EARLY"S DIVISION: (Walker)

	Commanding: Brig.Gen. James A. Walker

		JOHNSTON"S BRIGADE: (Lea)
		(4 N.C. Regts, 1 SS Bn)
		LEWIS' BRIGADE: (Beard)
		(4 N.C. Regts)
		WALKER"S BRIGADE: (Douglas)
		(5 Virginia Regts)

GORDON"S DIVISION: (Evans)

			Commanding: Brig.Gen. Clement A. Evans
		EVAN"S BRIGADE: (Lowe)	
			(6 Ga Regts, 3 Bn)
		TERRY"S BRIGADE: (Williams)	
			(13 Virginia Regts)
		YORK"S BRIGADE: (Waggaman)	
			(10 Louisiana Regts)
THIRD ARMY CORPS:			
	Commanding: Lt.Gen. A. P. Hill		
CORPS SUPPORT ELEMENTS:			
	Provost Guard:		
			5TH Alabama Bn.
MAHONE"S DIVISION:			
	Commanding: Maj.Gen. William Mahone		
		FORNEY"S BRIGADE:	
			(6 Alabama Regts)
		WEISIGER"S BRIGADE:	
			(5 Virginia Regts)
		HARRIS"S BRIGADE:	
			(4 Mississippi Regts)
		SORREL"S BRIGADE: (Tayloe)	
			(4 Ga Regts, 2 Ga Bn.)
		FINAGAN"S BRIGADE: (Lang)	
			(6 Florida Regts)
HETH"S DIVISION:			
	Commanding: Maj.Gen. Henry Heth		
		DAVIS" BRIGADE:	
			(4 Miss Regts, 1 CSA Regt)
		COOKE"S BRIGADE:	
			15th N.C. Regt
			27th N.C. Regt
			46th N.C. Regt
			48th N.C. Regt
			55th N.C. Regt
		MAC RAE"S BRIGADE:	
			(5 N.C. Regts)

		MC COMB"S BRIGADE:
		(8 Tenn Regts, 1 Md Bn)

WILCOX"S DIVISION:

	Commanding: Maj.Gen. Cadmus M. Wilcox	
		THOMAS" BRIGADE:
		(4 Georgia Regts)
		LANE'S BRIGADE:
		(4 N.C. Regts)
		MC GOWAN"S BRIGADE:
		(4 S.C. Regts)
		SCALES" BRIGADE: (Hyman)
		(5 N.C. Regts)

ANDERSON"S CORPS:

	Commanding: Lt.Gen. Richard H. Anderson

JOHNSON"S DIVISION:

	Commanding: Maj.Gen. Bushrod R. Johnson
	WALLACE"S BRIGADE:
	(5 S.C. Regts)
	MOODY"S BRIGADE:
	(3 Ala Regts, 1 Bn)
	WISE"S BRIGADE: (Goode)
	(4 Virginia Regts)
	RANSOM"S BRIGADE:
	(5 N.C. Regts)

CAVALARY CORPS:

	Commanding: Maj.Gen. Fitzhugh Lee	
		MUNFORD"S BRIGADE:
		(4 Virginia Regts)
		PAYNE"S BRIGADE:
		(3 Va Regts, 1 Bn)
		GARY"S BRIGADE:
		3 Regts Va, SC, Ga; 1 Legion)

W.H.F. LEE"S DIVISION:

	Commanding: Maj.Gen. W.F.C. Lee	
		BARRINGER"S BRIGADE:
		(4 N.C. Regts)

			BEALE"S BRIGADE: (Burt)	
			(4 Virginia Regts)	
			ROBERT"S BRIGADE:	
			(1 N.C. Regt, 1 Bn)	

ROSSER"S DIVISION:

		Commanding: Maj.Gen. Thmoas L. Rosser	
		DEARING"S BRIGADE:	
			(3 Virginia Regts, 1 Bn)
		MC CAUSLAND"S BRIGADE:	
			(4 Virginia Regts)

ARMY ARTILLERY:

FIRST CORPS ARTILLERY:

SECOND CORPS ARTILLERY:

THIRD CORPS ARTILLERY:

ANDERSON"S CORPS ARTILLERY:

HORSE ARTILLERY:

DEPARTMENT N.C. & SOUTHERN VIRGINIA - C.S.A.

	FIRST MILITARY DISTRICT: PETERSBURG DEFENSES:		
	Commanding: Brig,Gen. Henry A. Wise		
			(2 Va Bn, Hood Bn)
			(2d Class Militia)
			(Indp Signal Corps)

DEPARTMENT OF RICHMOND - C.S.A.

	Commanding: Lt.Gen. Richard S. Ewell	

G.W.C. LEE"S DIVISION:

	Commanding: Maj.Gen. G.W.C. Lee	
	BARTON"S BRIGADE:	
		(3 Va Regts, 2 Bn)
	MOORE"S BRIGADE:	
		(3 Va Res/LD Regts, 2 Bn)
	LOCAL DEF TRPS/RES BRIGADE:	
		(1 Res Regt, 6 Bn)
	ARTILLEY DEFENSE BRIGADE:	
		(9 Bn)

THE BATTLE LINE FOR PETERSBURG. 1864-5
VIRGINIA

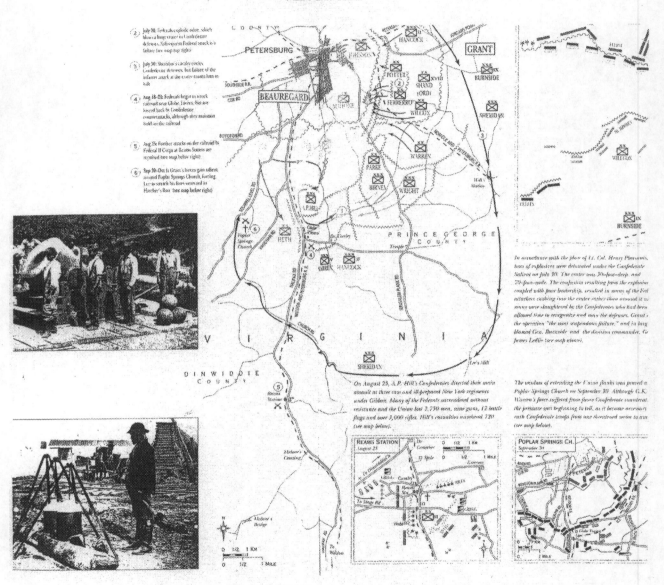

RE: THE ATLAS OF THE CIVIL WAR
M-11

Appromattox, Virginia—
The Retreat and Final Surrender . . .

CHAPTER XII.

The death march to Appomattox.

"On March 26th, 1865 Major-General Phil Sheridan's powerful cavalry command, under orders from Grant, crossed the James River and rode towards Petersburg. The movement, which threatened to unhinge the right flank of the Richmond-Petersburg defense system, was thwarted temporarily on March 31st when a Confederate force under Major-General George E. Pickett drove Sheridan's cavalry back from Dinwiddie Courthouse. Pickett then retired to Five Forks, where a defensive position was established to anchor the extreme right of Lee's line. On April 1st, Federal infantry and cavalry surprised Pickett at Five Forks and drove a wedge between his force and the Confederate line at Hatcher's Run. Pickett's men were then overpowered and driven from the field with heavy casualties, and an advance was opened to the flank and rear of Petersburg defenses. On April 2nd the Federals launched an attack against the Confederate line, broke through to the left of Cooke's brigade, and swept down the trenches. Cooke's men fell back to the second line of defenses, where they were subjected to infantry and artillery fire. General Lee, convinced that Richmond could no longer he held, ordered a general evacuation that night." 1

"The Army of North Virginia began retreating westward toward Amelia Courthouse on the evening of April 2nd. On April 4-5 the weary and half-starved Confederates, under hit-and-run attack by Federal cavalry, reached Amelia Courthouse, only to learn that the vital supplies ordered sent there ad not arrived. At Saylor's Creek the next day the rear guard of the army was cut off and largely destroyed, with the loss of approximately . . . . ?

General Robert E. Lee, General-in-chief of Confederate Forces was forced to surrender his Army of Northern Virginia [without food, water and ammunition] at Appomattox on April 9th under a flag of truce to General Grant.

General Grant under terms, granted a general amesty to the army and permitted them to return to their homes and families, to await proper exchange and pardon.

The 15 Officers and 102 men, survivors of the 46th Regiment North Carolina State Troops boarded a train with other North Carolinians for the trip southward to Raleigh, and onward to their home counties. The War was over for them!

Post script: From 1865 to 1896, General Hall continued in public & civil service—after serving as County Sheriff for several terms, became Chief of Police in 1875 and acting Mayor of Wilmington 1881, and Mayor in 1886 until his death in June 11th, 1896. In the State Convention of 1894, he became the Major-General and North Carolina State Commander of the United Confederate Veterans.

The Road to Appomattox APRIL 2–9 1865

After evacuating Richmond and Petersburg during the night of April 2–3, Confederate forces moved on multiple routes toward a junction at Amelia Court House on the Richmond and Danville Railroad. There Lee hoped to be resupplied before marching south into North Carolina to join General Jospeh Johnston's forces. Reaching Amelia on April 5, Lee united his columns but found no rations. He also learned that Grant's vigorous pursuit had placed large forces across his path near Jetersville, eight miles west of Amelia. Looping around the Federal concentration in an exhausting night march, Lee continued westward toward Farmville on the South Side Railroad. There he hoped to be supplied by rail from Lynchburg. Grant followed, sending II and VI Corps behind the Confederates while the cavalry and the V Corps, plus elements of the Army of the James, attempted to turn Lee's

pressed the rear of Lee's dwindling army. Surrounded at last by overwhelming force, Lee opened negotiations with Grant which resulted in the surrender of the Army of Northern Virginia at Appomattox Court House on the afternoon of April 9, 1865. This surrender brought the war in Virginia to an end.

Robert E. Lee photographed at his Richmond home in the uniform which he had worn when surrendering the Army of Northern Virginia a few days earlier (right). Lee disliked being photographed and the scarcity of likenesses had resulted in his being represented in newspapers throughout the war as dark haired and, apart from a black moustache, clean shaven. Such portrayals were based upon the general's appearance when he was a professor at West Point.

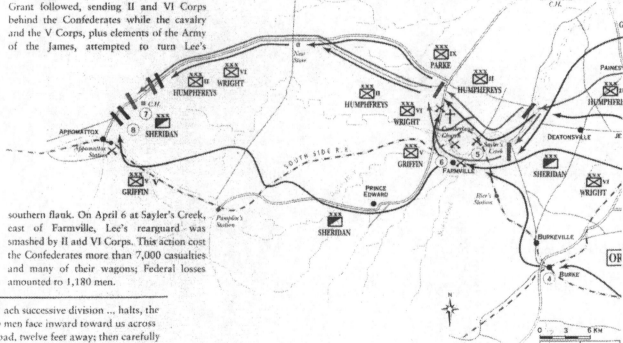

southern flank. On April 6 at Sayler's Creek, east of Farmville, Lee's rearguard was smashed by II and VI Corps. This action cost the Confederates more than 7,000 casualties and many of their wagons; Federal losses amounted to 1,180 men.

"Each successive division ... halts, the men face inward toward us across the road, twelve feet away; then carefully 'dress' their line... lastly... they tenderly fold their flags, battle-worn and torn, bloodstained, heart-holding colors, and lay them down; some frenziedly rushing from the ranks... pressing them to their lips with burning tears. And only the flag of the Union greets the sky!"

Gen. Joshua L. Chamberlain describing the surrender of the Confederate army. April 12, 1865.

THE ATLAS OF THE CIVIL WAR
M-12

REGIMENTAL CASUALTIES 1861-1865

CHAPTER XIII.

46th North Carolina Regimental Casualties: 1861-1865

(Narrative Battlefield Estimates and Reports)

BATTLES	Killed	Wounded	Missing	POWs
Richmond: (Malvern Hill)	?			
Sharpsburg:	5	60*	?	00*
Fredericksburg:	11	57		?*
Bristoe Station:	8	52*	00*	00*
Wilderness: (Eff: 540)	39	251*	0,000*	0?*
Spotsylvania:	?	000*	*?	0?*
Cold Harbour	?			
Richmond: (Reams Sta.)	00	000*	00*	0?*
Petersburg: (Hatcher's Run)	00	000*	0,000*	00?*
(Appomattox's	00	000	000	00)

Total Present at Surrendered: 118

Keynotes unknown numbers—?
Keynotes greatest source of POW's—*
Re: Summary of combined sources ?

No POW List has been found to date.
(See National Archives NC Microfich Roll for Individuals)

None recorded or found, reunion may have occurred as part of original organization of the NC United Confederate Veterans meeting.

REGIMENTAL BIOGRAPHICAL SKETCHES . . .

CHAPTER XIV.

The First Regimental Commander:
COLONEL Edward Dudley Hall, PACS

Edward Dudley Hall was a native of North Carolina born 1823. He graduated from Donaldson Academy in 1841. Being the son of a planter, the Honorable John Pearsall Hall of an Albemarle Plantation, began his career by entering state politics. Initially, elected to the State Legislature, first as a Representative, and later as Senator. Eventually, became involved in local politics—of the Cape Fear section, ran for Sheriff of New Hanover County, County seat Wilmington, and was heartily elected. His first wife, Susan Lane (died from Smallpox in 1862) while the family was residing in Wilmington during the war. Sheriff Hall, being quiet concerned for the state's safety, set about privately with his own funds recruiting about 100 men, and organizing them into a Heavy Artillery Company of local New Hanover Irishmen, calling themselves the "Rifle Ranges;" all of this occurred prior to North Carolina succeeding on May 20, 1862.

He enlisted into his own company as a private. The Artillery Company was offered to the State Adjutant General and mustered on 16 April 1861 into the state's military forces and was designated initially as Company H of the 3rd North Carolina Artillery, State Troops. Lacking artillery pieces and equipment, the unit was assigned to the 2nd North Carolina Infantry, State Troops on 2 June 1861 at Camp Mangum, near Raleigh. Company H Artillery was converted to Company A Infantry, and Private Hall was elected Captain Hall and company commander. The 2nd Regiment was deployed to the east to meet the Federal Army's invasion from the Atlantic coast. Captain Hall fought valiantly with his company and was cited for personal bravery at the Battle of New Bern.

Upon the organization of the 7th North Carolina Infantry, State Troops, (again at Camp Mangum) Captain Hall was transferred and elected Major of the Field & Staff of the 7th Regiment on 17 August 1861. The State needing experienced commanders, Major Hall was transferred and elected Colonel of the newly organized 46th North Carolina Infantry, State Troops on 4 April 1862.

Shortly, thereafter, the 46th Infantry was mustered into Confederate Service for 3 years, and promptly reassigned to Richmond, Virginia. Upon its arrival at Camp Lee, the regiment was required to boaster Richmond defenses, and assigned to Dewey's Bluffs overlooking the James River. On 31 May 1862 while in position, it was formed up the 27th NC, 48th NC, 3rd Ark, 30th Va and the 3rd Ga Battalion, and placed under the command of Brig.Gen. John G. Walker, to be known as Walker's Brigade. The brigade took part in the battle for Malvern Hill, and retired back to Richmond defenses.

Soon the unit was assigned to General Lee's Army of Northern Virginia, and placed in Longstreet's Corps, Walker's Division, and Manning's Brigade. COL Hall lead his regiment in the Maryland Campaign, ending in the battle for Sharpsburg, where he was again cited for a heroic charge! On 28 Oct 1862, the regiment was joined by the 15th NC, when Brig.Gen. Cooke took command of the Brigade; then realigned with Ramson's Division, it took part in the victorious Battle of Fredericksburg on 13 December 1862.

Before the Pennsylvania Campaign and upon departing winter quarters in 1863, Ramson's Division was sent south to assist the 3rd Military District, Department of SC-GA-FL to protect the north-south rail line at Pocataligo Station, South Carolina until 10 April 1863.

Upon returning to Richmond the brigade was reassigned to ANV, A.P. Hill's (Early) Corps, Heth's Division. On 3 Oct 1863 the army went into the victorious battle of Bristoe Station. The unit later retired to winter quarters for 1864.

COL Hall retired home to await his promotion to Brigadier General and a new command. In the meantime, he was reelected to County Sheriff. He felt a greater need for the defenses of Wilmington and under took to command the Militia. The Last great fortification—Fort Fisher and the City of Wilmington surrendered to Federal forces on 15 Jan 1865. General Hall was immediately put under house arrest till the end of the war, which in North Carolina occurred on 20 April 1865. In 1866, he would later run as a democratic candidate for Lieutenant Governor, and again put under house arrest by Federal authorities. Finally, he would serve as the Major-General, Commanding the Department of North Carolina, United Confederate Veterans until his death on 11 June 1896.

The First Regimental Sergeant-Major:
SERGEANT-MAJOR Thomas Settle Troy

Sergeant Troy had previously resided in Randolph County, enlisted at Newton, NC where he was a student. At the age of 22, he mustered with the Company G of the 46th North Carolina Infantry Regiment. He was promoted to Regimental Sergeant-Major on 1 May 1862. Upon a vacancy in Company G, he was elected 2nd Lieutenant on 3 February 1863 and stepped down as senior NCO of the regiment (transferred back to Company G to resume duties as an officer). He served the regiment honorably prior to be killed at the Battle of the Wilderness on 5 May 1864.

46th North Carolina Infantry Regiment, CSA
COPYRIGHT ACKNOWLEDGEMENTS

Reprinted with the permission of the following sources:

1. Cover Page—COL Hall's Photo: Confederate Veteran, SCV-UCV Mag.: 1896.
2. Cover Page—Enlistment Poster: Library of Congress, Wash., DC 2005.
3. Map 1 Page—NC: NC State Archives, Raleigh, NC 2005.
4. Poster Page - Enlistment Poster: Library of Congress, Wash., DC 2005.
5. Flag Page—Confederate Flags: Page xvi = LOC 2005.
6. Organizational Page - 46th NC: The National Archives, Wash., DC 2005.
7. COL Hall's Photo—Confederate Veteran, SCV-UCV Mag: 1896.
8. 46th NC F&S Photo: NC State Archives, Raleigh, NC 2005.
9. Map 2 Page—Central VA: Illustrated Atlas of the CW by Time-Life Books @ 1996 by Time-Life Books Out of Print.
10. Map 3 Page 9—Malvern Hill, VA: ibid.
11. Table 1 Pages 10-12 = OB CSA Malvern Hill, VA: ibid.
12. Map 4 Page 17 - Sharpsburg, MD: ibid.
13. Table 2 Page 18-20 = OB CSA Sharpsburg, MD: ibid.
14. Map 5 Page 23—Fredericksburg, VA: ibid.
15. Map 5a Page 24—BF Fredericksburg, VA, CWPT, Wash. DC 2005.
16. Table 3 Pages 25-27 = OB CSA Fredericksburg, VA: Illustrated Atlas of the CW by Time-Life Books @ 1996 by Time-Life Books Out of Print.
17. Map 6 Page 34 = Bristoe Station, VA: ibid.
18. Map 7 Page 37 = Wilderness, VA: ibid.
19. Table 4 Pages 38-40 = OB CSA Wilderness, VA: ibid.
20. Map 8 Page 42—Spotsylvania, VA: ibid.
21. Map 9 Page 45—Cold Harbour, VA: ibid.
22. Map 10 Page—Richmond, VA: ibid.
23. Table 5 Pages 46-50 = OB CSA Richmond, VA: ibid.
24. Map 11 Page 60 = Petersburg, VA: ibid.
25. Table 6 Pages 54-58 = OB CSA Petersburg, VA: ibid.
26. Map 12 Page 63 = Appomattox, VA: ibid.
27. Roster 1 Pages 72-122: The National Archives, Wash., DC 2005
28. Roster 2 Pages 123-125: ibid.
29. Map 13 Page—Railroads of the Confederate States, 1861 by Wiley I. Bell, The Embattled Confederates; Harper and Roe Co., New York, NY: 1964.

APPENDICIES

COMPLIED SERVICE RECORDS OF THE CONFEDERATE SOLDIERS

(Extracts)

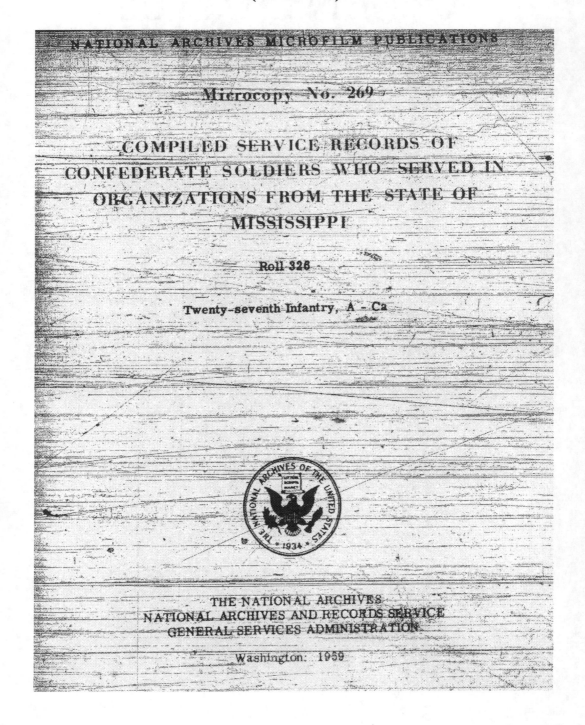

NATIONAL ARCHIVES MICROFILM PUBLICATIONS

Microcopy No. 269

COMPILED SERVICE RECORDS OF
CONFEDERATE SOLDIERS WHO SERVED IN
ORGANIZATIONS FROM THE STATE OF
MISSISSIPPI

Roll 326

Twenty-seventh Infantry, A - Ca

THE NATIONAL ARCHIVES
NATIONAL ARCHIVES AND RECORDS SERVICE
GENERAL SERVICES ADMINISTRATION

Washington: 1959

Hall. Edward. D.

Co. ___, 46 North Carolina Inf.
F & S.

(Confederate.)

Colonel | Colonel

CARD NUMBERS.

1	4886565	20	
2	5678	21	
3	5690	22	
4	5705	23	
5	5554	24	
6	78300	25	
7	8094	26	
8		27	
9		28	
10		29	
11		30	
12		31	
13		32	
14		33	
15		34	
16		35	
17		36	
18		37	
19		38	

Number of medical cards herein _____

Number of personal papers herein _____

BOOK MARK: _____

See also *2nd Regt N C Inf and*
7th Regt N C Inf

REGISTER OF COMMISSIONED OFFICERS AND NON-COMMISSIONED OFFICERS, FORTY-SIXTH REGIMENT NORTH CAROLINA VOLUNTEERS

(Roster 1)

ALPHABETIC INDEX NAME- TWENTY SEVENTH MISSISSIPPI INFANTRY REGIMENT, VOLUNTEERS							
LAST NAME	FIRST NAME	MI	RANK	POSITION	Footnotes	Page	Ref: 4
Hall	Edward	D.	Brigadier-General	Commander	Transferred		
Saunders	William	L.	Colonel	Commander			
Enkins	William	A.	Lieutenant-Colonel	Executive Officer	Resigned		
McAllister	Alexander	C.	Lieutenant-Colonel	Executive Officer	Transferred		
Mitchell	Rush	J.	Major		Resigned		
Norment	Richard	M.	Major		Resigned		
McNeill	Neill	M.	Major				
Mallett	Richardson	Jr.	Staff (3d Lieut.)	Adjutant	Killed		
Mitchell	Lucio		Staff (2d Lieut.)	Adjutant	Resigned		
Small	Robert	S.	Staff (1st Lieut.)	Adjutant (Acting)			
Owens	Thomas		Staff ((3d Lieut.)	Adjutant (Acting)			
Green	Simon	T.	Staff	Surgeon	Resigned		
Piggot	William	M.	Staff	Surgeon	Relieved		
Jenkins	E.	M.	Staff	Surgeon	?		
West	G.	S.	Staff	Surgeon	Relieved		
Thompson	Vines	O.	Staff	Asst Surgeon			
Hussey	Thomas	C.	Staff	Hospital Steward			
Cohen	Abraham	D.	Staff	Chaplain	Resigned		
Dodson	Charles	C.	Staff	Chaplain	Resigned		
Marsh	James	A.	Staff (Captain)	Asst Quartermaster			

Waddell	John	M.	Staff (Sergeant)	Quartermaster	Transferred		
Carroll	James	L.	Staff (Sergeant)	Quartermaster			
Shell	Oliver	P.	Staff (Sergeant)	Commissaries	Transferred		
Leach	James	A.	Staff (Acting)	Commissaries	?		
Holmes	Gabriel		Staff (Captain)	Asst Comm. Subs.	Transferred		
McCotter	Richard	D.	Staff (Sergeant)	Ordnance Sgt.	Prom 3d Lt		
Tucker	Jessie	D.	Staff (Sergeant)	Ordnance Sgt.			
Hammond	John		Staff (1st Lieut.)	Ensign	Resigned		
Troy	Thomas	S.	Sergeant-Major		Prom 2d Lt		
			Sergeant-Major		Transferred		
Leach	James	A.	Sergeant-Major	(Acting)	Relieved		
Wright	Thomas	H.	Sergeant-Major				
Sutton	Plummer		Drillmaster		Resigned		
Heflin	Henry	H.	Band	Chief Musician			
Haynes	George	M.	Band (Drummer)	Musician			
Yoder	Marcus		Band (Drummer)	Musician			
Arnold	John		Band	Musician	Dropped		
Beckerdite	John	T.	Band	Musician	POW		
Hampton	Wiley	P.	Band	Musician			
Jackson	Wiley	C.	Band	Musician			
McBryde	James	A.	Band	Musician			
McPhaul	Malcom	J.	Band	Musician			
Miller	John		Band	Musician			
Riddle	Charles	W.	Band	Musician			
Rodgers	Charles	W.	Band	Musician			
Smith	William	J.	Band	Musician			
Teague	Alpheus	A.	Band	Musician			
COMPANY - A	Robeson	NC	Lumberton Guards	Infantry	8/2/1862		
Norment	Richard	M.	Captain	Commander	4/4/1862		
COMPANY - B		NC	Rifles	Infantry			
Saunders	William	L.	Captain	Commander	4/4/1862		
COMPANY - C		NC	Rifles	Infantry			
Jones	Stephen	W.	Captain	Commander	4/4/1862		
COMPANY - D		NC	Sons of Mars	Infantry			
Stewart	Colin		Captain	Commander	4/4/1862		
COMPANY - E		NC	Tar River Rebels	Infantry			

Heflin	Robert	L.	Captain	Commander	4/4/1862		
COMPANY - F		NC	Rifles	Infantry			
McAllister	Alex	C.	Captain	Commander	4/4/1862		
COMPANY - G		NC	Randolph Rangers	Infantry			
Carr	Obed	W.	Captain	Commander	4/4/1862		
COMPANY - H		NC	Moore Guards	Infantry			
McNeill	Neill	M.	Captain	Commander	4/4/1862		
COMPANY - I		NC	Coharie Guards	Infantry			
Holmes	Owen		Captain	Commander	4/4/1862		
COMPANY - K		NC	Catawba Guards	Infantry			
Bost	Adolphus	T.	Captain	Commander	4/4/1862		
RANK and FILE:							

COMPLETE REGIMENTAL MUSTER ROSTER OF OFFICERS AND MEN SERVING FROM 1861 THRU 1865

(Roster 2)

ALPHABETIC INDEX NAME—FORTY-SIXTH NORTH CAROLINA INFANTRY VOLUNTEERS				
First Name	Last Name	Company	Rank_In	
Caleb	Abernathy	K	Private	Private
John P.	Abernathy	K	Fifer	Private
Miles	Abernathy	K	Private	Musician
John Q.	Adams	G	Private	Private
John Quincy	Adams	G	Private	Private
Nathaniel	Adams	F	Private	Private
Nathaniel T.	Adams	F	Private	Private
George P.	Adcock	E	Private	Corporal
William A.	Adcock	E	Musician	Private
Woodward A.	Adcock	E	Musician	Private
A. F.	Agner	B	Private	Private
John F.	Agner	B	Private	Private
Joseph	Aiken	E	Private	Private
John A.	Aldridge	G	Private	Private
William	Alford	B	Private	Private
Daniel	Allen	F	Private	Private
Squire	Anderson	E	Private	Private
Turner	Armstrong	K	Private	Private
John E.	Arney	K	Private	Private
Philip E.	Arney	K	Private	Private
John	Arnold	H	First Sergeant	Private
Neill T.	Arnold	H	Sergeant	Sergeant
William	Arnold	H	Private	Private
Henry	Arnts	K	Private	Private
Jacob E.	Arnts	K	Private	Private
Henry	Arntz	K	Private	Private

Jacob	Arntz	K	Private	Private
W.	Aropest	K	Private	Private
Allen M.	Aughtry	I	Private	Private
Phillip	Aughtry	I	Private	Private
Henry	Aurnt	K	Private	Private
Jacob	Aurnt	K	Private	Private
Jacob	Aurntz	K	Private	Private
Allen M.	Autrey	I	Private	Private
Philip	Autrey	I	Private	Private
Allen M.	Autry	I	Private	Private
Philip	Autry	I	Private	Private
Thomas M.	Avaris	C	Private	Private
J. H.	Babbitt	C	Private	Private
Josiah	Baggett	I	Private	Private
Matthew R.	Baggett	A	Private	Private
James H.	Bagley	I	Private	Private
William C.	Bain	G	Sergeant	Corporal
Presley W.	Baldwin	F	Private	Private
William H.	Baldwin	F	Private	Private
James D.	Ball	G	Private	Private
James A.	Ballard	A	Private	Private
Jesse J.	Balthrop	C	Private	Private
Jacob W.	Bandy	K	Private	Private
William C.	Bane	G	Sergeant	Corporal
D. P.	Bannell	H	Private	Private
Alex S.	Barden	I	Private	Corporal
Allen S.	Barden	I	Private	Corporal
Andrew	Barger	B	Private	Private
C.A.	Baringer	B	Private	Private
Isaac N.	Barker	G	Private	Private
Thomas C.	Barlette	C	Private	Private
Amos	Barns	G	Private	Private
A.M.	Barringer	B	Private	Private
Perry R.	Barringer	K	Private	Private
R.P.	Barringer	K	Private	Private
Leroy L.	Bartlett	C	Private	Private
C.A.	Basing	B	Private	Private
A. Caleb	Basinger	B	Private	Private
Caleb A.	Basinger	B	Private	Private
Eli	Basinger	B	Private	Private

George	Basinger	B	Private	Private
J. W.	Basinger	B	Private	Private
Joseph	Basinger	B	Private	Private
Monroe	Basinger	B	Private	Private
Richard	Bass	D	Private	Private
Willis	Bass	I	Private	Private
J. M.	Bassinger	B	Private	Private
James J.	Bates	B	Private	Private
J. J.	Bathrop	C	Private	Private
Stephen	Baxley	A	Private	Private
E.	Bayner	G	Private	Private
Justus	Beach	B	Private	Private
John T.	Beal	H	Private	Private
Richard T.	Bean Jr.	F	Private	Private
Richard T.	Bean Sr.	F	Private	Private
James C.	Beasley	D	Private	Private
A. T.	Beat	H	Private	Private
Jesse	Beaver	B	Private	Private
John P.	Beaver	B	Private	Private
David B.	Beckerdite	G	Sergeant	Sergeant
John T.	Beckerdite	G	Private	Musician
John G.	Beddingfield	A	Private	Private
Calton	Bedsole	H	Private	Private
Duncan	Bedsole	H	Private	Corporal
William	Bedsole	H	Private	Private
Henry	Bell	G	Private	Private
George D.	Bellamay	C	Private	Sergeant
J. W.	Bellamay	C	Private	Private
John W.	Bellamey	C	Private	Private
George D.	Bellamy	C	Private	Sergeant
John W.	Bellamy	C	Private	Private
Lee	Bennett	G	Private	Private
L.	Bennitt	G	Private	Private
John W.	Bettamy	C	Private	Private
David	Birchett	E	Private	Private
Elisha H.	Birkhead	F	Corporal	Corporal
John	Birmingham	A	Private	Private
Alfred	Bishop	C	Private	Private
Fred	Black	G	Private	Private
Philip	Black	G	Private	Private

William F.	Blair	G	Private	Private
Calvin	Blake	H	Private	Private
J. R.	Block	H		
Duncan F.	Blue	H	Private	Private
John A. B.	Blue	H	Second Lieutenant	First Lieutenant
Joseph H.	Bobbitt	C	Private	Private
Marshal	Bodiford	A	Private	Private
Stephen	Bodiford	A	Private	Private
Uriah	Bodiford	A	Private	Private
William P.	Bollinger	K	Corporal	Corporal
Frank S.	Bondurant	C	Private	Private
T. S.	Bondurant	C	Private	Private
Thomas	Books	G	Private	Private
James Monroe	Boovy	K	Private	Private
Marcus A.	Boovy	K	Private	Private
Miles M.	Boovy	K	Private	Private
Silas B.	Boovy	K	Private	Private
Adolphus T.	Bost	K	Captain	Captain
Alfred W.	Bost	K	Private	Private
John J.	Bost	B	Private	Private
Moses A.	Bost	B	Private	Private
Robert A.	Bost	K	Private	Captain
William H.	Bost	B	Private	Private
Andrew J.	Bowden	C	Private	Private
John Owen	Bowden	G	First Sergeant	Private
Robert	Bowden	C	Private	Private
Thomas	Bowden	C	Private	Private
W. T.	Bowden	C	Private	Private
Andrew J.	Bowdon	C	Private	Private
Robert	Bowdon	C	Private	Private
Upton T.	Bowdon	C	Private	Private
John B.	Bowen	C	Private	Private
Robert	Bowen	C	Private	Private
Samuel	Bowles	E	Private	Private
Stephen	Boxley	A	Private	Private
Marcus	Boyd	K	Private	Private
R. Winfield	Boyd	K	Private	Private
Robert W.	Boyd	K	Private	Private
Winfield R.	Boyd	K	Private	Private
Solomon	Boykin	I	Sergeant	Sergeant

R.	Bracket	C	Private	Private
Charles	Braday	H	Private	Private
A.	Bradchen	E	Private	Private
Charles	Braddy	H	Private	Private
Addison	Bradshaw	E	Private	Private
John R.	Bradshaw	I	Private	Private
Adison	Bradsher	E	Private	Private
Charles	Brady	H	Private	Private
E.	Branch	A	Private	Private
James	Branch	B	Private	Private
L. E.	Branch	I	Private	Private
Lucian C.	Branch	I	Private	Private
Manuel	Branch	A	Private	Private
R. A.	Brandon	B	Private	Private
Isaac N.	Branson	F	Private	First Sergeant
Thomas A.	Branson	F	Second Lieutenant	Captain
Hansweh	Braswell	C	Private	Private
Addison	Bratcher	E	Private	Private
Edward J.	Bray	G	Private	Private
A. M.	Brench	A	Private	Private
R.	Bresnell	F	Private	Private
Henry	Brewer	H	Private	Private
Sampson	Brewer	H	Private	Private
Wesley	Brewer	H	Private	Private
William	Brewer	H	Sergeant	Sergeant
Alexander	Briggs	E	Private	Private
Wellington	Brigman	A	Private	Private
Walter J.	Brinkley	E	Private	Private
Wiley	Brinkley	E	Private	Private
Benjamin S.	Britt	A	Private	Private
Ignatious W.	Brock	G	Private	First Lieutenant
J. H.	Brock	G	Private	Private
R.	Brock	G	Private	First Lieutenant
John P.	Brooks	H	Private	Private
Martin V.	Brooks	G	Private	Private
Thomas	Brooks	G	Private	Private
James M.	Brower	F	Private	Private
W. B.	Brower	G	Private	Private
W. Preston	Brower	G	Private	Private
William P.	Brower	G	Private	Private

Willis L.	Brower	G	Private	Private
James	Brown			
John	Brown	F	Private	Private
John D. A.	Brown	B	Private	Private
Joshua	Brown	D	Private	Private
Willis	Brumble	A	Private	Private
Richard B.	Bryan	A	Private	Private
A.	Bryant	E		
John A.	Buchanan	A	Private	Private
W. O.	Buchanan	C	Private	Private
William O.	Buckhannon	C	Private	Private
Benjamin	Bullard	A	Musician	Private
Daniel	Bullard	H	Private	Private
Elgate P.	Bullard	A	Private	Private
Elseph	Bullard	A	Private	Private
James A.	Bullard	A	Private	Private
Henry A.	Bullock	E	Private	Private
James T.	Bullock	E	Private	Private
William G.	Bullock	E	Private	Private
Aram	Bumgarner	K	Private	Private
Hosea L.	Bumgarner	K	Private	Private
Durham P.	Bundles	H	Private	Private
J. W.	Bundy	K	Private	Private
Durham P.	Bunnell	H	Private	Private
Jehu	Bunten	G	Private	Private
John	Bunting	G	Private	Private
William R.	Burch	K	Private	Private
David	Burchard	E	Private	Private
Franklin F.	Burgess	G	Private	Private
E.	Burgin	F	Corporal	Corporal
Brooks T.	Burke	H	Private	Private
T. B.	Burke	H	Private	Private
John C.	Burns	A	Private	Private
Alfred L.	Burriss	G	Private	Private
J.	Buthrop	C	Private	Private
Aaron	Butler	D	Private	Private
James	Butler	G	Private	Private
Jefferson	Butler	G	Private	Private
John	Butler	I	Private	Private
Tristian	Butler	D	Private	Private

William	Butler	D	Private	Private
William	Butler	I	Private	Private
James H.	Bynum	C	Private	Private
William E.	Bynum	C	Private	Private
James H.	Byrum	C	Private	Private
William E.	Byrum	C	Private	Private
Archibald C.	Cadwell	D	Private	Private
Jacob P.	Caison	I	Private	Corporal
A. C.	Caldwell	D	Private	Private
Henry H.	Caldwell	K	Private	Private
George W.	Califer	E	Private	Private
Arch M. D.	Cameron	H	Private	Private
Benjamin F.	Cameron	H	Private	Private
John A.	Cameron	H	Private	Private
Neill G.	Cameron	H	Private	Private
Neill J.	Cameron	H	Private	Private
B. F.	Cammeron	H	Private	Private
J. A.	Cammeron	H	Private	Private
Alexander	Campbell	A	Private	Private
Daniel	Campbell	D	Private	Private
Henry A.	Campbell	D	Private	Private
Neill	Campbell	D	Private	Private
J.	Canada	I	Private	Private
John R.	Canady	I	Private	Private
Thomas J.	Capps	C	Private	Private
Warren H.	Capps	C	Sergeant	Sergeant
Obed William	Carr	G	Captain	Captain
James L.	Carroll	I	Private	Quartermaster Sergeant
John	Carter	I	Private	Private
John L.	Carter	F	Private	Private
Josiah L.	Carter	F	Sergeant	Sergeant
McElvany C.	Carter	I	Private	Private
Newton	Carter	F	Private	Private
Thomas A.	Carter	C	Private	Private
William H.	Carter	I	Private	Private
Patrick	Casey	E	Private	Private
Robert W.	Cates	E	Private	Private
Joel M.	Causey	H	Private	Private
Joel W.	Causey	H	Private	Private

Joshua C.	Causey	H	Private	Private
Benjamin S.	Caveness	G	Private	Private
G.R.	Caveness	G	Private	Private
Isaac F.	Caveness	G	Private	Corporal
John R.	Caveness	G	Private	Private
William J.	Caveness	G	Private	Private
John R.	Caviness	G	Private	Private
J.F.	Caviniss	G	Private	Corporal
W.J.	Caviniss	G	Private	Private
J.F.	Cavness	G	Private	Corporal
W.J.	Cavness	G	Private	Private
David	Chandler	B	Private	Private
Samuel W.	Cheek	G	Private	Private
A.J.	Cherry	B	Private	Private
George P.	Childers	K	Private	Private
John C.	Childers	K	Private	Private
William	Clap	F	Private	Private
B.F.	Clark	C	Private	Private
B.M.	Clark	C	Private	Private
B.T.	Clark	C	Private	Private
Broomfield	Clark	C	Private	Private
Madison	Clark	H	Private	Private
A.J.	Clarry	B	Private	Private
A.J.	Clary	B	Private	Private
Andrew J.	Clery	B	Private	Private
Amon	Cline	K	Private	Private
William P.	Cline	K	Private	Private
George W.	Clodfelter	K	Private	Private
Calvin M.	Cobb	K	Private	Private
Henry H.	Cogwell	K	Private	Private
A.D.	Cohen		Chaplain	Chaplain
James N.	Cole	A	Private	Private
John D.	Cole	C	Private	Private
John W.	Cole	A	Private	Private
Willis	Cole	F	Private	Private
David	Collins	C	Private	Private
Henry T.	Collins	H	Private	Private
Adam	Comer	H	Private	Private
Zebedee F.	Comer	I	Private	Private
J. Wilborn	Conner	F	Private	Private

Joseph W.	Conner	F	Private	Private
Welborn	Conner	F	Private	Private
Zebedee	Conner	F	Private	Private
William Payton	Coon	B	Private	Sergeant
Andrew J.	Cooper	I	Private	Private
Thomas	Cooper	I	Private	Private
Dwight A.	Council	A	Private	Private
Henry P.	Covington	D	Private	Private
Samuel	Covington	D	Private	Private
Daniel H.	Cox	G	Private	Private
F.H.	Cox	G	Private	Private
L.H.	Cox	G	Private	Private
Brodie	Cozart	E	Corporal	Private
Thomas G.	Cozart	E	Private	Private
P.C.	Cranford	B	Private	Private
G.N.	Crarer	B	Private	Private
Benton H.J.	Craven	F	Private	Private
F.	Craven	F	Sergeant	Sergeant
George H.	Craven	G	Private	Private
J. Austin	Craven	G	Private	Private
Jeremiah F.	Craven	F	Sergeant	Sergeant
Robert P.	Craven	F	Private	Private
Samuel J.	Craven	G	Private	Private
P.C.	Crawford	B	Private	Private
John	Crawley	B	Private	Private
J.	Crewley	B	Private	Private
James A.	Crews	E	Sergeant	Sergeant
Zeral	Crowder	C	Private	Private
Solomon	Crump	A	Private	Private
W.E.	Crumple	I	Private	Private
William E.	Crumpler	I	Private	Private
Alexander B.	Currie	D	Sergeant	Sergeant
Archibald C.	Currie	H	First Sergeant	Private
Duncan J.	Currie	H	Corporal	Sergeant
W. A. M.	Curry	B	Corporal	Corporal
A. Randolph	Curtis	G	Private	Private
J.	Curtis I	I	Private	Private
Henry	Dagerhart	K	Private	Private
Harold	Daniel	C	Private	Private
Daniel	Darroch	H	Private	Private

Daniel	Darrock	H	Private	Private
Archibald	Davis	H	Private	Private
B.	Davis	F	Private	Private
Duncan	Davis	F	Private	Private
Emory	Davis	H	Private	Private
George W.	Davis	D	Private	Private
George W.	Davis	H	Private	Private
James	Davis	A	Private	Private
James	Davis	G	Private	Private
James R.	Davis	A	Private	Private
James W.	Davis	E	Corporal	Sergeant
John L.	Davis	G	Private	Sergeant
Joseph C.	Davis	G	Corporal	Sergeant
R. G.	Davis	A	Private	Private
Richard J.	Davis	A	Private	Private
Samuel W.	Day	E	Private	Private
Henry	Deagarheart	K	Private	Private
Miles M.	Deal	K	Private	Private
William L.	Deator	K	Private	Private
Mills	Denton	B	Private	Private
W. L.	Detter	K	Private	Private
Edward W.	Dickerson	E	Private	Private
Whitwell	Dickerson	E	Private	Private
W.	Dickson	E	Private	Private
David J.	Dillard	A	Private	Private
David J.	Dilliard	A	Private	Private
James	Dilliard	A	Private	Private
Nelson	Dixon	E	Private	Private
C.C.	Dobson	F&S	Chaplain	Chaplain
C.C.	Dodson	F&S	Chaplain	Chaplain
G.P.	Dodson	G	Private	Musician
Virgil S.	Dorsett	G	Private	Private
Neill	Douglass	D	Private	Private
Rufus	Draper	A	Private	Private
George W.	Drum	K	Private	Private
Haldelona	Duke	E	Private	Private
Noah	Duke	E	Private	Private
Robert	Duke	E	Private	Private
William C.	Duke	C	Private	Private
William K.	Duke	E	Private	Corporal

George W.	Duncan	E	Commissary of Subsistence	Private
Nicholas	Dunn	A	Private	Private
William	Dunn	B	Private	Private
William	Dunn	H	Private	Private
Joseph S.	Dunn, Jr.	F	Sergeant	Private
James H.	Dupree	G	Private	Private
Ransom	Eades	K	Private	Private
Ransom	Eads	K	Private	Private
David	Eagle	B	Private	Private
Eli	Earnhardt	B	Private	Private
Eli	Earnhart	B	Private	Private
Abel S.	Eckard	K	Private	Private
Able S.	Eckerd	K	Private	Private
Simon	Eckerd	K	Corporal	Sergeant
J.E.	Edwards	C	Private	Private
James M.	Edwards	C	Private	Private
Jesse A.	Edwards	G	Private	Private
Joseph G.	Edwards	C	Private	Private
Robert	Edwards	C	Sergeant	Sergeant
Samuel T.	Edwards	C	Private	Private
Abel S.	Ekard	K	Private	Private
Simon	Ekard	K	Corporal	Sergeant
Simon	Ekerd	M	Corporal	Sergeant
Benjamin J.	Ellington	E	Private	Private
Meredith G.	Ellington	C	Private	Private
James D.	Ellingtonc	C	Private	Private
J.	Ellis	E	Private	Private
Jeremiah	Ellis	E	Private	Private
Thomas	Ellis	E	Private	Private
A.A.	Ellison	F	Private	Private
Albert H.	Ellison	F	Private	Private
Alexander	England	B	Private	Private
Thomas M.	Evans	C	Private	Private
G.B.	Ezrell	I	Private	Private
Henry F.	Ezzell	I	Private	Private
James E.	Ezzell	I	Corporal	Sergeant
John B.	Ezzell	I	Private	Private
Michael J.	Ezzell	I	Private	Private
J.	Faircloth	I	Private	Private

Jacob	Faircloth	I	Private	Private
James	Faircloth	I	Private	Private
Stephen	Faircloth	A	Private	Private
Zachariah	Faircloth	I	Private	Private
Alexander F.	Falkener	C	Private	Private
John W.	Falkener	C	Private	Corporal
Alexander	Falkner	C	Private	Private
John W.	Falkner	C	Private	Private
William	Farr	B	Private	Private
Alexander	Faulkner	C	Private	Private
John W.	Faulkner	C	Private	Private
W. S.	Ferabow	E	Private	Private
Monroe	Ferebow	E	Private	Private
William S.	Ferebow	E	Private	Private
Archabold	Fergeson	H	Private	Private
D. M.	Fergeson	H	Private	Private
Ferges	Fergeson	H	Private	Private
Peter	Fergeson	H	Private	Private
William	Fergeson	H	Private	Private
Archa	Fergueson	H	Private	Private
Fergus	Fergueson	H	Private	Private
Peter	Fergueson	H	Private	Private
William	Fergueson	H	Private	Private
Archibald	Ferguson	H	Private	Private
Daniel M.	Ferguson	H	Private	Private
Fergis	Ferguson	H	Private	Private
James	Ferguson	H	Private	Private
John A.	Ferguson	H	Private	Private
Larkin	Ferguson	G	Private	Private
Peter	Ferguson	H	Private	Private
William	Ferguson	H	Private	Private
Monroe	Ferobow	E	Private	Private
W. S.	Ferobow	E	Private	Private
M.	Ferribault	E	Private	Private
W.	Ferribault	E	Private	Private
A. A.	Fhipps	B	Private	Private
D.	Field	C	Corporal	Private
George W.	Field	C	Corporal	Private
George	Fields	C	Corporal	Private
Peter	Fields	F	Private	Private

Hardie H.	Figer	G	Private	Private
John H.	Finch		Private	Private
Daniel	Finger	K	Private	Private
Doctor F.	Finger	K	Private	Private
Franklin	Finger	K	Private	Private
A. A.	Fipps	B	Private	Private
Micajah J.	Flanagan	C	Private	Private
M. J.	Flangan	C	Private	Private
M. J.	Flanigan	C	Private	Private
George H.	Fleming	C	Private	Corporal
Jacob D.	Fleming	C	Private	Private
Nathan N.	Fleming	B	First Lieutenant	Captain
Henry	Floid	F	Private	Private
John	Floid	F	Private	Private
Henry	Flowers	A	Private	Private
Pinkney	Flowers	A	Private	Corporal
Henry H.	Floyd	F	Private	Private
Henry M.	Floyd	F	Private	Private
John	Floyd	F	Private	Private
Squire	Floyd	G	Private	Private
Zimri	Floyd	G	Private	Private
M.	Forbes	G	Private	Private
Monroe	Forbis	G	Private	Private
Robert H.	Ford	C	Corporal	Second Lieutenant
John	Forsyth	E	Private	Private
Alexander H.	Fortner	C	Private	Private
John W.	Fortner	C	Private	Private
Merada	Fouler	D	Private	Private
William H.	Foust	G	Corporal	Corporal
Isaac	Fowler	E	Private	Private
Merada	Fowler	D	Private	Private
Morasda	Fowler	D	Private	Private
N.	Fowler	D	Private	Private
George W.	Fox	G	Private	Private
S. M.	Fox	G	Private	Private
Samuel	Fox	G	Private	Private
H.	Franklin	K	Private	Private
Wesley	Franklin	B	Private	Private
H.H.	Frazer	G	Private	Private
H.A.	Frazier	G	Private	Private

Hardie H.	Frazier	G	Private	Private
W.D.B.	Freeland	G	Private	Private
Aaron	Freeman	F	Private	Private
Enoch	Freeman	H	Private	Private
Joseph G.	Freeman	E	Private	Private
Joseph H.	Freeman	A	First Sergeant	Second Lieutenant
Nathaniel D.	Freeman	E	Private	Private
David	Freeze	B	Private	Private
Joel M.	Freeze	B	Private	Private
John	Frick	B	Private	Private
M.	Frick	B	Private	Private
David	Frieze	B	Private	Private
Joel M.	Frieze	B	Private	Private
George	Frutter	F	Private	Private
Calvin G.	Fry	K	Private	Private
Jacob	Fry	K	Private	Private
John A.D.	Fry	K	Private	Private
Alpheus C.	Fuller	E	Musician	Private
Archie	Furgerson	H	Private	Private
William	Furgurson	H	Private	Private
Archibald	Furguson	H	Private	Private
Daniel M.	Furguson	H	Private	Private
James	Furguson	H	Private	Private
John A.	Furguson	H	Private	Private
Peter	Furguson	H	Private	Private
Thomas A.J.	Futral	G	Private	Sergeant
Junius L.	Gaither	K	Private	Private
James	Ganatt	C	Private	Private
Levi	Gant	K	Private	Private
Thomas	Gantier	I	Private	Private
A.C.	Gardner	B	Private	Private
Charles	Gardner	B	Private	Private
James	Gardner	B	Private	Private
Thomas P.	Gardner	C	Private	Private
William	Gardner		Private	Private
Enoch	Garner	F	Private	Private
Jackson	Garner	F	Private	Private
James	Garner	B	Private	Private
James	Garrett	C	Private	Private
James	Garrott	C	Private	Private

Joseph N.	Gault	K	Private	Private
Levi	Gault	K	Private	Private
Levi	Gaunt	K	Private	Private
Thomas	Gautier	I	Private	Private
Sidney	Gerrald	F	Private	Private
Hampton	Ghee	B	Private	Musician
Abner H.	Gheen	B	Private	Musician
H.A.	Gheen	B	Private	Private
Milas A.	Gheen	B	Private	Private
P.H.	Gheen	B	Private	Musician
C.C.	Ghilson	H	Lieutenant	Lieutenant
Enoch	Gibson	F	Private	Private
Stephen P.	Gibson	D	Private	Private
T.	Gibson	A	Private	Private
T.J.	Gibson	A	Private	Private
Zimri	Gibson	A	Private	Private
Philip V.	Gilbert	K	Private	Private
David J.	Giles	I	Private	Private
John W.	Gilleland	C	Private	Sergeant
John W.	Gilliland	C	Private	Sergeant
John	Gillilin	C	Private	Sergeant
Charles	Glovel	A	Private	Private
Charles	Glover	A	Private	Private
Roby J.	Glover	A	Private	Private
Charles C.	Goldston	H	Lieutenant	First Lieutenant
B.	Gooch	C	Private	Private
Paul	Gooch	E	Private	Private
Radford	Gooch	E	Private	Private
William T.	Gooch	E	Private	Private
Christopher	Goodman	A	Private	Private
Columbus	Goodman	K	Private	Private
G.	Goodman	K	Private	Private
George	Goodman	B	Private	Private
John T.	Goodman	D	Private	Private
J. H.	Gordy	G	Private	Private
J. W. H.	Gordy	G	Private	Private
Moses	Gordy	G	Private	Private
E. Rowland	Goss	E	Private	Private
Esquire R.	Goss	E	Private	Private
Simeon	Goss	E	Private	Corporal

William	Goss	E	Private	Private
Thomas	Gotier	I	Private	Private
James	Grady	B	Private	Private
Alexander M.	Graham	D	Private	Private
Daniel A.	Graham	H	Private	Private
James C.	Graham	D	Private	Private
James H.	Graham	D	Corporal	Corporal
N. M.	Graham	D	Private	Private
William	Graham	H	Private	Private
Noah	Graves	F	Private	Private
Zebedee	Graves	F	Private	Private
J. C.	Grayham	D	Private	Private
Simon T.	Green		Surgeon	Surgeon
William	Green	G	Private	Private
J. M.	Gregory	B	Private	Private
John N.	Gregory	B	Private	Private
James T.	Grisham	E	Private	Private
Charles H.	Grissom	E	Private	Private
James T.	Grissom	E	Private	Private
P. H.	Grisson	E	Private	Private
Thomas	Groom	E	Private	Private
A.	Grubb	G	Private	Private
Louis D.	Gulley	A	Private	Private
Walter W.	Gulley	A	Private	Private
William W.	Gulley	A	Private	Private
William W.	Gulley	A	Private	Private
J.D.	Gurley	F	Private	Private
James	Gurley	F	Private	Private
William A.	Gurley	B	Private	Private
James J.	Hagood	C	Private	Private
James W.	Hagood	C	Private	Private
Bunyon	Hails	H	Private	Private
Giles	Hails	H	Private	Private
R.	Hails	A	Private	Private
Daniel	Hair	I	Private	Private
James D.	Hair	I	Private	Private
John	Hair	I	Private	Private
Stephen	Hair	I	Private	Private
Thomas E.	Hair	I	Private	Private
Wiley T.	Hair	I	Private	Private

Bunyan	Hales	H	Private	Private
Giles	Hales	H	Private	Private
Reddin	Hales	A	Private	Private
Edward D.	Hall	F&S	Colonel	Colonel
Humphrey	Hall	K	Private	Private
Lewis	Hall	H	Private	Private
Lucian J.	Hall	I	Corporal	First Sergeant
Lawson G.	Halshinser	B	Private	Sergeant
Haynes L.	Haman	A	Private	Private
John	Haman	A,C	Private	Sergeant
Stephen	Haman	A	Private	Private
Stradford	Haman	A	Corporal	Sergeant
Willis	Haman	A	Private	Private
Haynes L.	Hammond	A	Private	Private
John	Hammond	A,C	Private	Sergeant
Stephen	Hammond	A	Private	Private
Stradford	Hammond	A	Corporal	Sergeant
Willis	Hamond	A	Private	Private
John S.	Hampton	B	Private	Private
Wiley P.	Hampton	F&S	Private	Musician
J.W.	Hancock	F	Private	Private
Noah	Hancock	F	Private	Private
Wesley	Hancock	F	Private	Private
John	Hancock, Jr.	F	Private	Private
John	Hancock, Sr.	F	Private	Private
Jonathan	Hardin	A	Private	Private
J.	Hardy	A	Private	Private
Thomas	Hare	I	Private	Private
Christopher	Harkey	B	Private	Private
George A.	Harmon	G	Private	Sergeant
J.	Harntz	K	Private	Private
A. A.	Harris	C	Private	Private
Andrew	Harris		Private	Private
Andrew J.	Harris	E	Private	Private
Charles	Harris	E	Private	Private
Fielding	Harris	E	Corporal	Corporal
H. J.	Harris	E	Private	Private
Lewis A.	Harris	E	Private	Private
W. B.	Harris	C	Private	Private
William H.	Harris	C	Private	Private

Williamson G.	Harris	B	Private	Private
M. A.	Harrison	K	Private	Private
Charles C.	Harryman	B	Private	Sergeant
Jacob L.	Hartso	K	Private	Private
Marcus	Harverson	K	Private	Private
Marcus A.	Harvison	K	Private	Private
C. C.	Haryman	B	Private	Sergeant
Paul	Hashourer	B	Private	Private
John Martin	Hass	K	Private	Private
Colin	Hasty	D	Private	Corporal
John H.	Hasty	D	Private	Private
Robert A.	Hasty	D	Private	Private
Franklin	Havner	B	Musician	Private
J. F.	Havner	B	Musician	Private
William P.	Hawn	K	Private	Private
W. J.	Hayle	C	Private	Private
George Macon	Haynes	K	Drummer	Musician
Junius S.	Hays	E	Private	Sergeant
Junius H.	Hazer	E	Private	Sergeant
Jacob	Heartsoe	K	Private	Private
Charles E.	Heathcock	E	Private	Private
Henry H.	Heflin	E	Private	Musician
Jesse Franklin	Heflin	E	Second Lieutenant	Captain
Jesse R.	Heflin	E	Second Lieutenant	Captain
Robert Lewis	Heflin	E	Captain	Captain
G. M. G.	Heilig	B	Private	Private
Franklin A.	Helton	K	Private	Private
Hosea	Helton	K	Private	Private
William	Helton	K	Private	Private
Farley E.	Henderson	F	Private	Private
Hugh A.	Henderson	D	Private	Private
L. H.	Henderson	C	Third Lieutenant	Third Lieutenant
John	Hendren	A	Private	Private
Jacob	Hendricks	G	Private	Private
Jacob	Hendrix	G	Private	Private
Alexnader T.	Herring	I	Private	Sergeant
Giles	Herring	A	Private	Private
Isaiah	Herring	I	Sergeant	Second Lieutenant
John D.	Herring	I	Third Lieutenant	Second Lieutenant
Anderson	Hewit	K	Private	Private

Franklin A.	Hewit	K	Private	Private
John S.	Hewit	K	Private	Private
Joseph L.	Hewit	K	Private	Private
William L.	Hewit	K	Private	Private
H. G.	Hicks	C	Private	Private
Harrison	Hicks	G	Private	Private
John	Hicks	C	Private	Private
John	Hicks	G	Private	Private
Silas G.	Hicks	C	Private	Private
Thomas J.	Hicks	C	Private	Private
William	Hicks	K	Sergeant	Sergeant
William F.	Hicks	C	Private	Private
M.	Hier	I	Private	Private
Lewis W.	Highsmith	I	Private	Sergeant
S. W.	Highsmith	I	Private	Sergeant
Doctor H.	Hill	F	Private	Private
Hilliard	Hill	F	Private	Private
John C.	Hill	F	Private	Private
John L.	Hill	A	Private	Private
Samuel	Hill	F	Private	Private
Sion	Hill	G	Private	Private
William H.	Hill	F	Private	Private
William T.	Hill	G	Private	Private
Hilliard	Hill Jr.	F	Private	Private
James	Hilliard	C	Private	Private
W. H. H.	Hix	G	Private	Private
William H.	Hix	G	Private	Private
John	Hobbs	K	Private	Private
Lewis	Hobbs	F	Private	Private
James P.	Hobgood	E	Private	Private
J.	Hobson	K	Private	Private
Richard	Hodge	A	Private	Private
John	Holder	G	Private	Private
John W.	Holder	G	Private	Private
James	Holdshouser	B	Private	Private
L. G.	Holdshouser	B	Private	Sergeant
James	Holeman	A	Private	Private
Daniel	Holland	I	Private	Private
Henry Y. C.	Holland	I	Private	Private
Joel	Holland	I	Private	Private

James	Holman	A	Private	Private
Gabriel	Holmes	I	First Sergeant	Acting Commissary of Subsistence
Owen	Holmes	I	Captain	Captain
Benjamin	Holshouser	B	Private	Sergeant
F. M.	Holshouser	B	Private	Private
Jacob R.	Holshouser	B	Private	Private
James	Holshouser	B	Private	Private
Lawson G.	Holshouser	B	Private	Sergeant
O. M.	Holshouser	B	Private	Private
W. P.	Holshouser	B	Private	Private
Jacob W.	Holt	C	Private	Private
Bunyon	Holy	H	Private	Private
Eli	Honbarger	B	Private	Private
Jacob	Honbarger	B	Private	Private
Jacob	Honburger	B	Private	Private
Alexander	Honeycutt	B	Private	Private
Hiram	Honeycutt	I	Private	Private
Philip H.	Honeycutt	I	Private	Private
Hiram	Honycutt	I	Private	Private
Philip H.	Honycutt	I	Private	Private
William	Honycutt	I	Private	Private
James M.	Hoover	K	Second Lieutenant	Second Lieutenant
William Sidney	Hoover	K	Private	Private
George	Horah	B	Second Lieutenant	First Lieutenant
Rowan	Horah	B	Private	Private
Eli	Hornbarger	B	Private	Private
Jacob	Hornbarger	B	Private	Private
David S.	Howard	I	Private	Private
James A.R.	Howard	I	Private	Private
John T.	Howard	I	Private	Private
William O.	Howard	I	Private	Private
John J.	Howell	A	Private	Corporal
M.	Howison	K	Private	Private
John D.	Hoyle	C	Private	Private
Peter F.	Hoyle	G	Private	Private
William J.	Hoyle	C	Private	Private
H.M.	Huddleston	E	Private	Private
Marcellus	Huddleston	E	Private	Private

Samuel	Huddleston	E	Private	Private
Alfred	Hudson	I	Private	Private
Henry	Hudson	I	Private	Private
Solomon	Hudson	I	Private	Private
William M.	Hudson	I	Private	Private
Noah	Huffman	K	Private	Corporal
Samuel	Huffman	K	Private	Private
Banister A.	Hughes	E	Sergeant	Private
David A.	Hughes	E	Private	Private
Farley	Hughes	F	Private	Private
Jacob S.	Hughes	E	Private	Private
S.H.	Hughes	F	Private	Private
Solomon	Hughes	F	Private	Private
A.H.	Hughs	G	Private	Private
David	Hughs	G	Private	Private
H.S.	Hughs	F	Private	Private
Anderson	Huit	K	Private	Private
Franklin	Huit	K	Private	Private
Joseph L.	Huit	K	Private	Private
William	Huit	K	Private	Private
G. Washington	Hunt	G	Private	Private
George W.	Hunt	G	Private	Private
Leonard	Hunt	G	Private	Private
James D.	Hurley	B	Private	Private
Thomas C.	Hussey	G	Sergeant	Hospital Steward
Lewis W.	Hysmith	I	Private	Sergeant
Alphonso M.	Ingold	G	Private	Private
Eucepheus P.	Ingold	F	Private	Sergeant
Eusebeus P.	Ingold	F	Private	Sergeant
Eusebias P.	Ingold	F	Private	Sergeant
J.B.	Isell	I	Private	Private
Bartlett G.	Isenhour	K	Private	Private
David	Israel	A	Private	Private
Henry	Israel	A	Private	Corporal
J.L.	Israel	A	Private	Private
Lott	Israel	A	Private	Private
John L.	Isreal	A	Private	Private
Benjamin A.	Ivey	A	Private	Private
Claiborne	Ivey	A	Private	Private
Isham	Ivey	A	Private	Private

John Q.	Ivey	A	Private	Private
William H.	Ivey	A	Corporal	Corporal
Matthew E.	Jackson	I	Sergeant	Sergeant
Thomas	Jackson	G	Private	Private
Wiley C.	Jackson	I	Corporal	Musician
Wiley R.	Jackson	G	Private	Private
Obed M.	Jarett	K	Private	Private
O.M.	Jarratt	K	Private	Private
Addison L.	Jarrell	G	Private	Private
Samuel	Jarrell	F	Private	Private
Sidney	Jarrell	F	Private	Private
David	Jarrett	G	Private	Private
Obed M.	Jarrett	K	Private	Private
Charles E.	Jeffreys	E	Private	Private
Willis H.	Jeffreys	E	Private	Private
Charles E.	Jeffries	E	Private	Private
W.H.	Jeffries	E	Private	Private
E.M.	Jenkins	F&S	Surgeon	Surgeon
Madison Green	Jenkins	C	Private	Private
Thomas G.	Jenkins	C	Sergeant	Second Lieutenant
Thomas J.	Jenkins	C	Sergeant	Second Lieutenant
William A.	Jenkins	C	Captain	Lieutenant Colonel
Samuel	Jerral	F	Private	Private
Sidney	Jerral	F	Private	Private
Samuel	Jerrell	F	Private	Private
Sidney	Jerrell	F	Private	Private
Samuel	Jerrill	F	Private	Private
Sidney	Jerrill	F	Private	Private
Archibald	Johnson	D	Private	Private
Bethel A.	Johnson	G	Private	Private
Charles A.	Johnson	H	Private	Private
Daniel A.	Johnson	D	Private	Private
Daniel A.	Johnson	H	Private	Private
Dugald J.	Johnson	H	Corporal	Private
Enoch	Johnson	H	Private	Private
J. Oliver	Johnson	G	Private	Corporal
James	Johnson	B	Private	Private
Jesse	Johnson	A	Private	Private
John	Johnson	B	Private	Private

John B.	Johnson	H	Private	Private
Joseph O.	Johnson	G	Private	Corporal
Malcolm C.	Johnson	H	Sergeant	Private
Samuel	Johnson	H	Private	Private
William	Johnson	B	Private	Private
William G.	Johnson	E	Private	Private
William H.	Johnson	G	Private	Private
James	Johnston	B	Private	Private
John	Johnston	B	Private	Private
William	Johnston	B	Private	Private
Calvin	Jones	H	Private	Private
Calvin R.	Jones	F	Private	Private
Duncan	Jones	D	Private	Private
F. H.	Jones	E	Private	Private
Hiram	Jones	D	Private	Private
James H.	Jones	D	Private	Private
John A.	Jones	K	Private	Private
John C.	Jones	H	Private	Private
R. K.	Jones	A	Sergeant	Private
Richard R.	Jones	A	Sergeant	Private
Samuel	Jones	D	Private	Private
Stephen W.	Jones	C	Captain	Captain
Thomas H.	Jones	E	Private	Private
Charles S.	Jordan	I	Private	Private
Enoch	Jordan	F	Private	Private
I. P.	Joyce	A	Private	Private
Thomas P.	Joyce	A	Private	Private
G. W.	Julian	G	Private	Private
John T.	Julian	G	Private	Private
Abram	Justice	B	Private	Private
B.	Justice	B	Private	Private
Lawson	Justice	B	Private	Private
Abram	Justus	B	Private	Private
Lawson	Justus	B	Private	Private
D. S.	Kanup	B	Private	Private
S. W.	Kearnes	G	Private	Private
S.	Kearns	G	Private	Private
Silas W.	Kearns	G	Private	Private
Alexander L.	Keener	K	Private	Private
James W.	Keener	K	Private	Private

Silas W.	Keerans	G	Private	Private
Duncan	Kellehan	A	Private	Private
Daniel	Kelly	D	Private	Private
John	Kelly	D	Corporal	Sergeant
David I.	Kemp	B	Private	Private
Daniel	Kennedy	E	Private	Private
J.	Kennedy		Private	Private
J. R.	Kennedy	I	Private	Private
Kendrick K.	Kennedy	F	Private	Sergeant
S. R.	Kennedy	I	Private	Private
William	Kennedy	F	Private	Private
David S.	Kenup	B	Private	Private
S. W.	Kerans	G	Private	Private
John	Kerf	B	Private	Private
J. L.	Kestler	K	Private	Private
Samuel E.	Killian	K	Private	Private
Bartholemew	Kimball	C	Private	Private
John S.	Kimball	C	Private	Private
William D.	Kimball		Corporal	Sergeant
George W.	Kindley	G	Private	Private
Alexander L.	King	K	Private	Private
Armistead	King	C	Private	Private
Charles H.	King	C	Private	Private
Michael S.	King	I	Private	Private
Richard	King	E	Private	Private
Robert P.	King	C	Private	Private
Samuel	King	C	Private	Private
Jacob	Kinley	G	Private	Private
Z.	Kinley	G	Private	Private
Joseph R.	Kinton	E	Private	Private
James J.	Kirkland	C	Private	Private
W. J.	Kirkland	C	Private	Private
William W.	Kirkland	C	Private	Private
J. J.	Kirklin	C	Private	Private
J. Larkin	Kistler	K	Private	Private
John D.	Kistler	K	Private	Private
John L.	Kistler	K	Private	Private
Jacob	Klutts	B	Private	First Sergeant
Jeremiah	Klutts	B	Private	Private
Tobias	Klutts	B	Private	Private

D.S.	Knup	B	Private	Private
Wilie	Knup	B	Private	Private
J.L.	Kritter	K	Private	Private
A.	Kuhner	K	Private	Private
John	Kurff	B	Private	Private
Wilson	Lackey	F	Private	Private
Isaac	Lafevers	K	Sergeant	Sergeant
Israel	Lahon	H	Private	Private
L.	Lain	B	Private	Private
William	Lain	B	Private	Private
E.C.	Lamb	F	Private	Private
Urban C.	Lamb	F	Private	Private
James W.	Lamont	D	Private	Private
William H.	Lancaster	C	Private	Private
Lafayette	Lane	B	Private	Private
W. Frank	Lane	G	Private	Private
William	Lane	B	Private	Private
William P.	Laslie	B	Private	Private
John	Latham	F	Private	Private
Lawrence	Latham	F	Private	Private
Lewis	Latham	F	Private	Private
Henry C.	Latta	E	Private	Second Lieutenant
John	Lawes	F	Private	Private
John	Laws	F	Private	Private
Alexander McN.	Leach	D	Private	Private
James A.	Leach	G	Private	Private
E.W.	Ledwell	F	Private	Private
Wiley	Ledwell	F	Private	Private
Willis	Lee	F	Private	Private
Isaac	Lefevers	K	Sergeant	Sergeant
Henry	Leonard	K	Private	Private
Robert H.	Leonard	K	Private	Private
William	Leonard	A	Private	Private
W. P.	Leslie	B	Private	Private
Green H.	Lett	H	Private	Private
George M.	Levister	A	Private	Private
George W.	Levister	A	Private	Private
James M.	Lewis	I	Private	Private
Thomas	Lewis	B	Private	Private
W. H.	Lewis	F	Private	Private

William	Lewis	B	Private	Private
W.	Lindell	I	Private	Private
Jesse	Lindy	B	Private	Private
Andrew	Link	K	Private	Private
Thomas J.	Linn	B	Private	Private
George W.	Lloyd	C	Private	Private
Nathan	Lockaman	I	Private	Private
Robert O.	Lockaman	I	Private	Private
William H.	Lockaman	I	Private	Private
William N.	Lockaman	I	Private	Private
Nathan	Lockamy	I	Private	Private
William N.	Lockany	I	Private	Private
Nathan	Lockerman	I	Private	Private
Robert O.	Lockerman	I	Private	Private
W. N.	Lockman	I	Private	Private
William A.	Lockwood	I	Private	Private
Isaac R.	Lohon	H	Private	Private
John	Lorain	C	Private	Private
James	Lord	C	Private	Private
William B. A.	Lowrance	B	First Sergeant	Second Lieutenant
George W.	Loyd	C	Private	Private
James	Loyd	C	Private	Private
Joe G.	Loyd	C	Private	Private
Joseph A.	Loyd	C	Private	Private
William J.	Loyd	F	Private	Private
John H.	Lucas	B	Private	Private
John J.	Lucas	F	Private	Private
Sherrod	Lucas	I	Private	Private
Elijah	Luck	F	Private	Private
William	Luck	F	Private	Private
J. A.	Lucus	F	Private	Private
Henry L.	Luitz	K	First Sergeant	First Sergeant
John C.	Luitz	K	Private	Private
John R.	Luster	H	Sergeant	Sergeant
William	Luster	H	Private	Private
John C.	Lutes	K	Private	Private
Riley	Luther	F	Private	Private
J. C.	Lutz	K	Private	Private
Martin	Lyerly	B	Private	Private
Thomas J.	Lynn	B	Private	Private

Leon S.	Mabry	C	Private	First Lieutenant
Richard H.	Macon	C	Private	Private
C.	Maddows	E	Private	Private
A. G.	Magirt	D	Private	Private
C. M.	Mahaley	A	Private	Private
Charles	Mahaly	A	Private	Private
Lawrence	Mahaly	A	Private	Private
W. N.	Mahn	B	Private	Private
R.	Mallett	F&S	Adjutant	Adjutant
Willis	Malone	I	Private	Private
Reuben	Maness	G	Private	Private
Walter	Mangum	E	Private	Private
Wiley P.	Mangum	E	Private	Private
Dugald	Maples	H	Private	Private
Duncan T.	Maples	H	Corporal	Corporal
John M.	Maples	H	Private	Private
James A.	Marsh	F&S	First Lieutenant	Quartermaster
Henry J.	Marshall	C	Private	Private
Isham T.	Martin	C	Private	Private
Marion	Martin	K	Private	Private
S.	Math	C	Private	Private
Leonard S.	Maybury	C	Private	First Lieutenant
William N.	Mayhew	B	Private	Private
Alex C.	McAlester	F	Captain	Lieutenant Colonel
Alexander C.	McAlister	F	Captain	Lieutenant Colonel
Archibald	McArthur	D	Private	Private
John L.	McArthur	D	Private	Private
William	McArthur	H	Private	Private
James	McBride	D	Private	Private
James A.	McBride	HFS	Private	Musician
John A.	McBride	D	Private	Private
John M.	McBride	D	Private	Private
Joseph A.	McBride	D	Private	Private
James	McBryde	D	Private	Private
James A.	McBryde	H	Private	Musician
John A.	McBryde	D	Private	Private
John M.	McBryde	D	Private	Private
Joseph A.	McBryde	D	Private	Private

Matthew	McCallum	A	Private	Private
R. D.	McCatter	G.F	Private	Second Lieutenant
George	McClamb	I	Private	Private
J.	McClamb	I	Private	Private
Peter	McClean	H	Private	Private
Angus	McCloud	H	Private	Private
Duncan W.	McCormick	D	Private	Private
Edward R.	McCormick	D	Private	Private
James A.	McCormick	D	Private	Private
Richard D.	McCotter Jr.	G-F	Private	Second Lieutenant
R. D.	McCotton	G,F	Private	Second Lieutenant
Archibald	McCraney	H	Private	Private
Will R.	McCraney	H	Private	Private
Avery	McCurrie	B	Private	Private
W. A.	McCurrie	B	Private	Private
W. A.	McCurry	B	Private	Private
Angus	McDearmid	D	Private	Private
Angus	McDiarmid	D	Private	Private
Donald M.	McDonald	F	Private	Private
Donald W.	McDonald	F	Private	Private
William W.	McDonald	H	Private	Private
A.	McDougald	H	Private	Private
Riley	McDuel	G	Private	Private
M.	McElroy	I	Private	Private
Duncan	McFadyen	H	Private	Private
Duncan	McFayden	H	Private	Private
George W.	McGee	I	Private	Private
Joseph	McGeehee	E	Private	Private
Zach	McGeehee	E	Private	Private
Josiah	McGehee	E	Private	Private
Zachariah	McGehee	E	Private	Private
Joshua	McGehu	E	Private	Private
Zackariah	McGehu	E	Private	Private
Archibald G.	McGirt	D	Private	Private
Calvin	McGuirt	E	Private	Private
John F.	McKaly	C	Private	Corporal
Patrick	McKay	C	Private	Sergeant
Thomas	McKay	E	Private	Private
Hector	McKennon	H	Private	Private
Benjamin	McKenzie	I	Private	Private

Daniel J.	McKenzie	D	Private	Private
David S.	McKenzie	D	Private	Sergeant
Patrick	McKey	C	Private	Sergeant
Henry R.	McKinney	A	Second Lieutenant	Captain
H.R.	McKinnie	A	Second Lieutenant	Captain
Hector	McKinnon	H	Private	Private
David S.	McKuczick	D	Private	Sergeant
George	McLain	I	Private	Private
John A.H.	McLain	D	Private	Private
George	McLamb	I	Private	Private
Isham	McLamb	I	Private	Private
Minson	McLamb	I	Second Lieutenant	Second Lieutenant
William H.	McLamb	I	Corporal	Private
Isham	McLand	I	Private	Private
William H.	McLand	I	Corporal	Private
S.	McLane	A	Private	Private
Charles	McLean	D	Private	Private
Elias	McLean	A	Private	Private
John A.H.	McLean	D	Private	Private
John D.	McLean	D	Private	Private
Peter	McLean	H	Private	Private
Simeon	McLean	A	Private	Private
Calvin	McLemore	H	Private	Private
Angus	McLeod	H	Private	Private
Norman K.	McLeod	H	Private	Private
Duncan	McMillan	D	Private	Private
James	McMillan	D	First Sergeant	First Sergeant
James	McMillian	D	First Sergeant	First Sergeant
Franklin	McNeel	K	Private	Private
John	McNeely	B	Private	Private
H.A.	McNeil	H	Lieutenant	Second Lieutenant
Daniel	McNeill	H	Private	Private
Henry	McNeill	D	Corporal	Corporal
J.S.	McNeill	K	Private	Private
James F.	McNeill	K	Private	Private
John N.	McNeill	H	Private	Third Lieutenant
Neill A.	McNeill	H	Lieutenant	Second Lieutenant
Neill M.K.	McNeill	H	Captain	Major
Harry	McNiell	D	Corporal	Corporal
Archibald	McRae	D	Private	Private

Patrick	Mcoy	C	Private	Sergeant
Cornelius	Meadows	E	Private	Private
Hawkins	Meadows	E	Private	Private
Henderson	Meadows	E	Sergeant	Sergeant
James	Meadows	E	First Lieutenant	First Lieutenant
Lazarus	Meadows	E	Private	Private
Seth	Meadows	E	Private	Private
J. C.	Means	A	Corporal	Sergeant
Alva G.	Meares	A	Private	Private
Daniel B.	Meares	A	Private	Private
Dwight H.	Meares	A	Sergeant	Sergeant
Henry L.	Meares	A	Private	Private
John C.	Meares	A	Corporal	Sergeant
Hawkins	Meddows	E	Private	Private
Andrew	Medlen	H	Private	Private
Jacob	Medlen	H	Private	Private
James A.	Medlen	H	Private	Private
Shadrick	Medlen	H	Private	Private
Angus	Medlin	H	Sergeant	Sergeant
Jacob	Medlin	H	Private	Private
James A.	Medlin	H	Private	Private
Shadrach	Medlin	H	Private	Private
Andrew	Medlin Jr.	H	Private	Private
Henderson	Medows	E	Sergeant	Sergeant
J. F.	Mendechon	G	Private	Private
Julius	Mendenhall	G	Private	Private
J. F.	Mendennow	G	Private	Private
Noah	Mercer	A	Private	Private
Rowland	Mercer	A	Private	Private
J. W.	Merick	C	Private	Private
Bedford	Messimer	A	Private	Private
Hugh	Middleton	D	Second Lieutenant	Second Lieutenant
Aaron Wiley	Miller	B	Private	Private
B.	Miller	B	Private	Private
Daniel	Miller	B	Private	Private
David	Miller	B	Private	Private
David M.	Miller	A	Private	Private
Dempsey M.	Miller	F	Private	Private
Eli	Miller	B	Private	Private
G.	Miller	H	Captain	Captain

Jesse R.	Miller	K	Private	Private
John	Miller	K	Private	Musician
John D.	Miller	B	Private	Private
John Eli	Miller	B	Private	Private
Levi	Miller	B	Private	Private
William	Miller	B	Private	Private
Denton	Mills	B	Private	Private
C. A.	Misenheimer	B	Private	Private
C. A.	Misenhimer	B	Private	Private
C. A.	Misenhouser	B	Private	Private
C.	Misinhammer	B	Private	Private
John	Mitchell	E	Private	Sergeant
L.	Mitchell	F&S	Adjutant	Adjutant
R.J.	Mitchell		Major	Major
Fields B.	Moffitt	F	Private	Private
Hugh	Moffitt	G	Private	Private
Durell	Moize	E	Private	Private
Silas	Monk	E	Private	Private
Duncan M.	Monroe	H	Private	Private
Evander	Monroe	H	Private	Private
J. T.	Monroe	H		
Neill	Monroe	H	Private	Corporal
Thomas	Monroe	H	Private	Private
William E.	Monroe	H	Private	Private
William W.	Monroe	H	Private	Private
Joseph J.	Moodey	H	Private	Private
Joseph J.	Moody	H	Private	Private
John	Moon	G	Private	Private
J. F.	Moor	E	Sergeant	Private
G. W.	Moore	E	Private	Private
George N.	Moore	E	Private	Private
Henry	Moore	H	Private	Private
John W.	Moore	E	Private	Private
William P.	Moore	A	Private	Private
Daniel	Moose	E	Private	Private
Martin	Moose	K	Private	Private
William	Moose	K	Private	Private
James H.	Morgan	D	Private	Sergeant
Thomas W.	Morris	H	Private	Private
Daniel D.	Morriss	H	Private	Private

Martin	Morse	K	Private	Private
Henry W.	Moser	A	Private	Private
Benjamin L.	Moss	E	Private	Private
John F.	Moss	E	Sergeant	Private
Robert E.	Moss	E	Private	Private
Stephen M.	Moss	C	Private	Private
William H.	Mouser	K	Private	Private
Duncan M.	Munroe	H	Private	Private
Evander	Munroe	H	Private	Private
Neill	Munroe	H	Private	Corporal
Thomas	Munroe	H	Private	Private
William W.	Munroe	H	Private	Private
Anderson K.	Murphy	A	Private	Private
Malcomb	Myers	G	Private	Private
John H.	Myrick	C	Private	Private
John W.	Myrick	C	Private	Private
Orrel	Nailor	I	Private	Corporal
Abraham J.	Nance	G	Private	Private
H. A.	Nance	G	Private	Private
Isaac J.	Nance	G	Private	Private
J. J.	Nance	G	Private	Private
Thomas T.	Nance	G	Private	Private
William C.	Nance	F	Private	Private
Orrell	Naylor	I	Private	Corporal
Younged	Nead	A	Private	Private
William W.	Neal	C	Private	Private
J. P.	Newman	B	Private	Private
Ira P.	Newnam	B	Private	Private
James A.	Newnam	B	Private	Private
H. G.	Newton	C	Private	Private
Henry A.	Newton	C	Private	Private
James G.	Newton	C	Private	Private
James J.	Newton	C	Private	Private
John G.	Newton	C	Private	Private
Benjamin M.	Nicholson	C	Sergeant	First Sergeant
William A. J.	Nicholson	C	Second Lieutenant	First Lieutenant
Wyatt E.	Nicholson	C	Private	Private
Richard M.	Norment	A	Captain	Major
Daniel	Norton	D	Private	Private
J. J.	Norton	C	Private	Private

James	Norton	D	Private	Private
Loderick	Norton	D	Private	Private
Loderwick	Norton	D	Private	Private
Miles	Norton	D	Private	Private
Nelson	Norton	D	Private	Private
William L.	Norton	D	Private	Private
Robert M.	Norwood	K	Private	Corporal
Dolph W.	Oakley	E	Private	Private
Dolphin W.	Oakley	E	Private	Private
Duncan	Oakley	E	Private	Private
Hugh E.	Oakley	E	Private	Private
Hughenas	Oakley	E	Private	Private
John H.	Oakley	E	Private	Private
Kendall	Oakley	E	Private	Private
Robert H.	Oakley	E	Private	Private
Simon	Oakley	E	Private	Private
William J.	Oakley	E	Private	Private
James A.	Oates	H	Private	Sergeant
Doctor	Obriant	E	Private	Private
Zachariah H.	Obriant	E	Private	Private
Philip	Oldham	H	Private	Private
Alexander	Overcash	A	Private	Private
John J.	Overcash	A	Private	Private
Jonas W.	Overcash	A	Private	Private
Isaac Newton	Owen	G	Sergeant	Sergeant
John B.	Owen	I	Private	Private
Lucian	Owen	I	Private	Private
H. C.	Owens	B	Private	Private
Noah	Owens	F	Private	Private
Peter	Owens	F	Private	Private
Thomas	Owens	I	Private	Second Lieutenant
Benjamin R.	Palmer	C	Private	Private
James T.	Parham	E	Private	Private
James V.	Parham	E	Private	Private
Charles	Parker	K	Private	Private
James E.	Parker	G	Private	Private
John	Parker	K	Private	Private
Lemuel P.	Parker	K	Private	Private
Leonard	Parker	K	Private	Private
Samuel	Parker	K	Private	Private

Thomas H.	Parker	I	Private	Private
D. M.	Parks	B	Private	Private
David	Parks	B	Private	Private
Franklin	Parnell	A	Private	Private
Henry	Parnell	A	Private	Private
Oliver H.	Parsons	I	Private	Private
Cowper G.	Paschall	C	Private	Private
Louis B.	Paschall	C	Private	Private
Louis P.	Paschall	C	Private	Private
Robert A.	Paschall	C	Private	Private
William	Paschall	E	Private	Private
William J.	Paschall	C	Private	Private
Samuel	Pate	D	Private	Private
Thoroughgood	Pate	D	Private	Private
Malloy	Patterson	D	Second Lieutenant	Second Lieutenant
Neill Mc M.	Patterson	D	Private	Private
Neill Mc N.	Patterson	D	Private	Private
Rufus K.	Patterson	I	Musician	Private
C. J.	Patts	B	Private	Corporal
Coleman	Payne	K	Private	Private
Alexander	Peacock	F	Private	Private
Ephraim	Peacock	F	Private	Private
A.	Pearce	H	Private	Private
J.	Pearce	H	Private	Private
Zebedee	Pearce	G	Private	Private
James A.	Pearson	B	Second Lieutenant	First Lieutenant
James A.	Pearson	B	Private	Private
James T.	Pearson	B	Second Lieutenant	First Lieutenant
A.	Pecock	F	Private	Private
Ephraim	Pecock	F	Private	Private
Benjamin F.	Peebles	C	Private	Private
Thomas H.	Peebles	C	Private	Private
John	Peel	D	Private	Private
John J.	Peele	D	Private	Private
Monroe	Peeler	B	Private	Corporal
James	Peerce	H	Private	Private
William T.	Pegram	C	First Sergeant	First Sergeant
Archibald	Peirce	H	Private	Private
Doctor F.	Peirce	G	Private	Private
John	Peirce	H	Private	Private

A.	Peland	H	Private	Private
James	Pener	H	Private	Private
Paul	Peninger	A	Private	Private
Tobias	Penninger	B	Private	Private
Seth	Penny	E	Corporal	Private
William A.	Perdew	H	Private	Private
Henry	Perkins	K	Private	Private
Franklin	Pernell	A	Private	Private
Hardy	Perry	F	Private	Private
Robert D.	Pervis	D	Private	Private
Robert L.	Pervis	D	Private	Private
Rufus K.	Peterson	I	Musician	Private
Rufus	Peteson	I	Musician	Private
William J.	Pharris	D	Private	Private
Caswell	Phillips	A	Private	Private
Elias	Phillips	A	Private	Private
George W.	Phillips	A	Private	Private
Henry C.	Phillips	C	Private	Sergeant
Henry P.	Phillips	C	Private	Sergeant
Henry W.	Phillips	A	Private	Private
James A.	Phillips	A	Private	Private
L. C.	Phillips	A	Private	Private
Levi L.	Phillips	A	Sergeant	Sergeant
Noah R.	Phillips	H	Private	Private
Rhodes	Phillips	A	Private	Private
S. S.	Phillips	A	Private	Private
Samuel S.	Phillips	A	Private	Private
Sanders	Phillips	H	Private	Private
Washington L.	Phillips	A	Private	Sergeant
William	Phillips	A	Private	Private
Willis	Phillips	H	Private	Private
A. A.	Phipp	B	Private	Private
Archibald	Pierce	H	Private	Private
Doctor F.	Pierce	G	Private	Private
James	Pierce	H	Private	Private
John	Pierce	H	Private	Private
Zebedee	Pierce	G	Private	Private
Hugh	Pigg	B	Private	Private
William M.	Piggott	F&S	Surgeon	Surgeon
James W.	Piner	H	Private	Private

William J.	Piner	H	Private	Private
H. Washington	Pitman	A	Private	Corporal
Henry W.	Pitman	A	Private	Corporal
Jordan L.	Pitman	A	Private	Private
Anderson A.	Pittard	C	Private	Private
A. A.	Pittman	C	Private	Private
Jordan A. L.	Pittman	A	Private	Private
John A.	Pless	B	Private	Private
John L.	Pless	B	Private	Private
Marcus A.	Poovy	K	Private	Private
Miles M.	Poovy	K	Private	Private
Alexander	Pope	I	Private	Private
Willis H.	Pope	A	Private	Private
James H.	Porter	I	Private	Private
John H.	Porter	I	Private	Private
L. D.	Porter	H	Private	Private
Calvin G.	Potts	B	Private	Corporal
Calvin J.	Potts	B	Private	Corporal
Secrese	Powell	F	Private	Private
Moses C.	Powlas	B	Private	Private
Alfred L.	Presnell	F	Private	Sergeant
Allen	Presnell	F	Private	Private
Myron	Presnell	F	Private	Private
Nixon	Presnell	F	Private	Private
Rispeth	Presnell	F	Private	Private
T.P.	Presnell	F	Private	Private
Tilmon	Presnell	F	Private	Private
John	Prevatt	A	Private	Private
Thomas R.	Price	C	Corporal	Second Lieutenant
William	Priest	D	Private	Private
Thomas	Pritchard	F	Private	Private
John	Privett	A	Private	Private
John	Proctor	F	Private	Private
John	Propse	K	Private	Private
William	Propse	K	Private	Private
John	Propst	K	Private	Private
William	Propst	K	Private	Private
Robert L.	Purvis	D	Private	Private
George E.	Qualls	E	Private	Private
William H.	Qualls Jr.	E	Private	Private

William H.	Qualls Sr.	E	Private	Private
George	Quarles	E	Private	Private
William H.	Quarles	E	Private	Private
W. H.	Quarles St.	E	Private	Private
James	Rachaels	A	Private	Private
John	Rachels	D	Private	Private
Starling	Rachels	D	Private	Private
William	Rachels	D	Private	Private
William	Rachiels	D	Private	Private
John	Raechels	D	Private	Private
Sterling	Raechels	D	Private	Private
William	Raechels	D	Private	Private
D. M.	Raglan	E	Private	Private
Charles A.	Ragland	A	Private	Private
James M.	Ragland	E	Private	Private
John H.	Ragland	E	Private	Private
James M.	Ragling	E	Private	Private
John	Raichals	D	Private	Private
Starling	Raichals	D	Private	Private
William	Raichals	D	Private	Private
Daniel	Raines	G	Private	Private
Nathan	Raines	G	Private	Private
Marshall	Rayner	E	Private	Private
Annual	Reddick	G	Private	Private
Joseph	Reddick	G	Private	Private
Adam	Reep	K	Private	Private
Wallace A.	Reinhardt	K	Private	Private
David	Remer	B	Private	Private
David	Reynolds	F	Private	Private
David A.	Rhymer	A	Private	Private
David H.	Rhymer	A	Private	Private
David	Rich	B	Private	Private
Davis	Rich	G	Private	Private
John	Rich	B	Private	Private
Josiah	Rich	B	Private	Private
Robert	Rich	B	Private	Private
John	Richey	A	Private	Private
Abel	Riddle	H	Private	Private
Cato	Riddle	H	Private	Private
Daniel L.	Riddle	H	Corporal	Corporal

George W.	Riddle	H	Private	Musician
Hamilton H.	Riddle	H	Private	Private
Thomas	Riddle	H	Private	Private
Jersey B.	Rigan	C	Private	Private
George W.	Riggan	C	Private	Private
Gideon	Riggan	C	Private	Private
Jeremiah B.	Riggan	C	Private	Private
John G.	Riggan	C	Private	Private
Mingo E.	Riggan	C	Corporal	First Sergeant
Peter R.	Riggan	C	Private	Private
David	Rimer	B	Private	Private
Christian R.	Rinck	K	Private	Private
Christian R.	Rink	K	Private	Private
John	Ritchey	A	Private	Private
John	Ritchie	A	Private	Private
John	Rivers	C	Private	Private
Clarkson	Robbins	F	Private	Private
Franklin C.	Robbins	F	Private	Private
Isaac	Robbins	F	Private	Private
Nathan	Robbins	F	Private	Private
Elijah	Roberson	C	Private	Private
Hartwell	Roberson	C	Private	Private
Robert J.	Roberson	C	Private	Private
James W.	Roberts	C	Private	Private
Wiley P.	Roberts	E	Private	Private
Hartwell	Robertson	C	Private	Private
Robert J.	Robertson	C	Private	Private
J. K.	Robeson	B	Private	Private
A. K.	Robinson	B	Private	Private
A. R.	Robinson	B	Private	Private
Elijah	Robinson	C	Private	Private
H. Harrison	Robinson	K	Private	Private
Hartwell	Robinson	C	Private	Private
Henry H.	Robinson	K	Private	Private
Robert J.	Robinson	C	Private	Private
A. R.	Robison	B	Private	Private
Charles W.	Rodgers	C	Private	Musician
William	Rodgers	B	Private	Private
Charles W.	Rogers	C	Private	Musician
T. W.	Rogers	C	Private	Musician

William	Rogers	B	Private	Private
E.	Rollins	G	Private	Private
Isaac N.	Rollins	G	Private	Private
J. Newton	Rollins	G	Private	Private
S. N.	Rollins	G	Private	Private
John W.	Roper	D	Second Lieutenant	Second Lieutenant
Robert F.	Rose	C	Private	Private
Robert J.	Rose	C	Private	Private
William J.	Rose	C	Private	Private
William A.	Rottenbury	E	Private	Private
Alexander	Routh	K	First Lieutenant	Lieutenant
Levi W.	Routh	K	Sergeant	Sergeant
Alonzo H.	Rowe	K	Private	Private
J. Dallas	Rowe	K	Corporal	First Sergeant
Archibald	Royal	I	Corporal	Private
Hardy	Royal	I	Private	Private
Isham	Royal	I	Private	Private
J.	Royal	I	Private	Private
John	Royal	I	Private	Private
Matthew	Royal	I	Private	Private
Archibald	Royles	I	Corporal	Private
Archibald	Royls	I	Private	Private
William D.	Rudd	C	Private	Private
William W.	Rudd	C	Private	Private
P. A.	Rumple	B	Private	Private
T. A.	Rumple	B	Private	Private
Simpson	Russ	F	Third Lieutenant	Third Lieutenant
H. T.	Russell	F	Private	Private
John C.	Russell	E	First Sergeant	Second Lieutenant
T. H.	Russell	F	Private	Private
Thomas	Russell	F	Private	Private
Thomas C.	Russell	G	Private	Private
Thomas	Sanderson	A	Private	Sergeant
William L.	Saunders	B	Captain	Colonel
Francis V.	Schell	D	Private	Private
Francis V.	Scholl	D	Private	Private
John P.	Scott	A	Private	Private
Joseph	Scronce	K	Private	Private
Eli	Seaford	B	Private	Private
Henry A.	Seaford	B	Private	Private

Alexander	Seals	A	Private	Private
I.I.	Seats	K	Private	Private
John Q.	Seats	K	Private	Private
P.	Seats	F	Private	Private
Powell	Secrece	F	Private	Private
John Q.	Seitz	K	Private	Private
W.	Sessions	H	Private	Private
Arthur	Sessoms	I	Private	Private
Isaac	Sessoms	I	Private	Private
Isaiah	Sessoms	I	Private	Private
William	Sessoms	H	Private	Private
W.	Sessons	H	Private	Private
Arthur	Sessums	I	Private	Private
Isaac	Sessums	I	Private	Private
John A.	Settlemoir	K	Private	Private
John A.	Settlemyer	K	Private	Private
Calvin	Setzer	K	Private	Private
Carl	Setzer	K	Private	Private
Carr	Setzer	K	Private	Private
Daniel	Setzer	K	Private	Private
Daniel A.	Setzer	K	Private	Private
Wilborne S.	Setzer	K	Private	Private
Allen	Shadrach	E	Private	Private
Daniel J.	Shadrack	E	Private	Private
William B.	Shadrack	E	Private	Private
Armstead	Sharin	C	Private	Private
Joseph W.	Shaw	D	Private	Private
J.D.	Shearer	C	Private	Private
Armstead H.	Shearin	C	Private	Private
Armstead K.	Shearin	C	Private	Private
Drury	Shearin	E	Private	Private
John D.	Shearin	C	Private	Private
Nathaniel R.	Shearin	C	Private	Private
Nathaniel W.	Shearin	C	Private	Private
A.K.	Shearn	C	Private	Private
John D.	Shearn	C	Private	Private
Isaac	Sheffield	H	Private	Private
John	Sheffield	H	Private	Private
Jonathan	Sheffield	H	Private	Private
Oliver P.	Shell	C	First Sergeant	Private

114

Christopher	Sherrell	K	Private	Private
Christie H.	Sherrill	K	Private	Private
Henry	Sherrill	K	Private	Private
R.H.	Sherrill	K	Private	Private
Robert K.	Sherrill	K	Private	Private
Robert R.	Sherrill	K	Private	Private
Drury	Sherrin	E	Private	Private
Joseph	Shronce	K	Private	Private
Joseph	Shrouse	K	Private	Private
Isaac	Shuffield	H	Private	Private
Jonathan	Shuffield	K	Private	Private
D.P.	Shuford	A	Private	Private
John Sidney	Shuford	K	Sergeant	Second Lieutenant
Marcus C.	Shuford	K	Private	Corporal
William H.	Shuford	K	Corporal	Corporal
A.D.	Shuler	G	Private	Private
David	Shuler	G	Private	Private
Michael	Shuping	B	Private	Private
Levi	Sides	A	Private	Private
R.A.	Sides	B	Private	Private
Lafayette M.	Sigman	K	Private	Private
Lewis	Sigman	K	Private	Private
Marcus L.	Sigman	K	Private	Private
Reuben	Sigman	K	Private	Private
R.	Sigmon	K	Private	Private
James	Sikes	F	Private	Private
Evan	Simmons	I	Private	Corporal
Christopher T.	Simms	C	Private	Private
Ransom Harriss	Skeen	G	First Lieutenant	First Lieutenant
Daniel	Skipper	D	Private	Private
Murdock	Skipper	D	Private	Private
Abram	Sloop	B	Private	Private
Robert S.	Small	G	Sergeant	First Lieutenant
Alexander	Smith	A	Musician	Musician
Asariah F.	Smith	C	Private	Private
Benjamin	Smith	A	Private	Private
Calvin W.	Smith	A	Private	Private
Caswell	Smith	A	Private	Private
Daniel	Smith	H	Private	Private
Duncan	Smith	A	Private	Private

Halcome	Smith	H	Private	Private
Hector	Smith	H	Private	Private
Isaac	Smith	K	Private	Private
James	Smith	B	Private	Private
James W.	Smith	H	Private	Private
Joseph T.	Smith	A	Private	Corporal
K. R.	Smith	A	Corporal	Private
Malcom	Smith	H	Private	Private
O. C.	Smith	A	Private	Private
R. F.	Smith	C	Private	Private
Thomas R.	Smith	A	Corporal	Private
William A.	Smith	A	Private	Private
William J.	Smith	A	Corporal	Musician
William J.	Smith	H	Private	Private
Cicero M.	Smyer	K	Private	Private
George Walton	Smyer	K	Private	Private
J. W. S.	Smyer	K	Private	Private
John R.	Smyer	K	Private	Private
John W. L.	Smyer	K	Private	Private
Marcus A.	Smyer	K	Third Lieutenant	Third Lieutenant
Marcus N.	Smyer	K	Third Lieutenant	Third Lieutenant
Robert A.	Smyer	K	Private	Corporal
Walton G.	Smyer	K	Private	Private
L.	Smyre	K	Private	Private
Alexander K.	Snead	D	Private	Private
Younger	Snead	A	Private	Private
Kinith A.	Sneede	D	Private	Private
James A.	Sommers	A	Private	Private
Samuel M.	Southerland	C	Sergeant	First Lieutenant
Asa J.	Sowell	H	Private	Private
Abner H.	Spell	I	Private	Private
John	Spell	I	Private	Private
Owen	Spell	I	Private	Corporal
Owen	Spell	I	Private	Corporal
Robert L.	Spell	I	Private	Private
William	Spell	I	Private	Private
Addison	Spencer	F	First Sergeant	First Lieutenant
Edward C.	Spencer	F	Private	Private
Elan L.	Spencer	F	Private	Private
Esau L.	Spencer	F	Private	Private

Evans	Spencer	F	Private	Private
James Addison	Spencer	F	First Sergeant	First Lieutenant
Jesse	Spencer	F	Private	Private
Lemuel	Spencer	F	Private	Corporal
Nathan	Spencer	F	Corporal	Sergeant
Shubal E.	Spencer	F	Private	Private
Washington	Spencer	F	Private	Private
William	Spencer Jr.	F	Private	Corporal
John	Spiver	H	Private	Private
John	Spivey	H	Private	Private
Spencer	Spivey	H	Private	Private
Spencer	Spivy	H	Private	Private
John	Squires	C	Private	Private
Joseph	Sronce	K	Private	Private
James	Stallings	B	Private	Private
William P.	Stallings	C	Private	Private
James T.	Stark	E	Private	Private
William H.	Stark	C	Private	Corporal
John C.	Starnes	B	Private	Private
John C.	Stearn	B	Private	Private
J. C.	Stearnes	B	Private	Private
Benjamin F.	Steed	F	Sergeant	Private
McKinzie B.	Steed	G	Private	Private
W. P.	Steed	G	Private	Private
Winburn H.	Steed	G	Private	Private
E. P.	Stenson	G	Private	Private
Colin	Stewart	D	Captain	Captain
Daniel	Stewart	D	First Lieutenant	First Lieutenant
Duncan J.	Stewart	D	Private	Sergeant
James H.	Stewart	D	Private	Private
John J.	Stewart	B	Sergeant	Second Lieutenant
William	Stewart	D	Private	Private
W.	Stiles	B	Private	Private
William	Stiller	B	Private	Private
Eli P.	Stinson	G	Private	Private
John M.	Stinson	G	Private	Private
Robert Wiley	Stinson	G	Second Lieutenant	Second Lieutenant
Andrew J.	Stogner	D	Private	Private
Andrew	Stokes	H	Private	Private
Angus	Stokes	H	Private	Private

H. M.	Stone	H	Private	Private
R. T.	Stone	C	Private	Private
Robert F.	Stone	C	Private	Private
Henry M.	Stout	H	Private	Private
John M.	Stout	H	Private	Private
O. R.	Stout	H	Private	Private
Oliver	Stout	H	Private	Private
Oliver K.	Stout	H	Private	Private
William M.	Stout	H	Private	Private
Archibald L.	Stroud	E	Private	Private
George P.	Stroud	E	Private	Private
William C.	Stroud	E	Private	Private
James H.	Strum	E	Private	Sergeant
Silas	Stubbs	D	Private	Private
Wade H.	Stuton	A	Sergeant	Private
Joseph	Styers	A	Private	Private
William	Styles	B	Private	Private
Francis M.	Sullivan	G	Private	Private
Marion	Sullivan	G	Private	Private
James A.	Summey	A	Private	Private
Isaac L.	Summit	K	Private	Corporal
Pinkney	Summit	K	Private	Private
G.W.	Suratt	F	Private	Private
Gorrell W.	Surratt	F	Private	Private
Samuel M.	Sutherland	C	Sergeant	First Lieutenant
Oates	Sutton	I	Private	Sergeant
Plummer	Sutton		Drillmaster	
Wade H.	Sutton	A	Sergeant	Private
Harrison	Swink	B	Private	Private
Thomas C.	Tadlock	F	Private	Private
Thomas E.	Tadlock	F	Private	Private
William S.	Tadlock	I	Private	Private
John A.	Tart	I	Private	Private
Robert W.E.	Tate	C	Private	Private
George	Tatom	I	Private	Private
George	Tatoon	I	Private	Private
George	Tatum	I	Private	Private
Andrew J.	Taylor	B	Private	Private
Henry	Taylor	A	Private	Private
John	Taylor	A	Private	Private

John P.	Taylor	B	Private	Private
Stephen M.	Taylor	C	Private	Private
William W.	Taylor	A	Private	Private
A.J.	Taylor, Jr.	B	Private	Private
Alpheus A.	Teague	F	Private	Musician
Meredith M.	Teague	F	Corporal	Captain
Algernon	Teasley	E	Private	Private
William	Teasley	E	Private	Corporal
Silas	Teer	I	Private	
W.B.	Terrel	H	Private	Private
David	Terry	B	Private	Private
Thomas L.	Terry	B	Private	Private
William	Terry	B	Private	Private
George	Tetom	I	Private	Private
W.	Tetyre	K	Private	Private
Daniel	Tew	I	Private	Private
Daniel L.	Tew	I	Private	Private
Lewis	Tew	I	Private	Private
Richard	Tew	I	Private	Private
Silas	Tew	I	Private	Private
William C.	Thagart	H	Private	Private
W.C.	Thaggard	H	Private	Private
Ben S.	Thomas	C	Private	Private
J.W.	Thomas	C	Private	Private
James	Thomas	C	Private	Private
M.C.	Thomas	H	Private	Private
Mack	Thomas	H	Private	Private
Stephen M.	Thomas	D	First Lieutenant	First Lieutenant
Charles R.	Thomasson	E	Private	Private
Henry T.	Thomasson	E	Private	Private
Samuel	Thomasson	E	Private	Private
William	Thomasson	E	Private	Private
H.	Thomaston	E	Private	Private
William	Thomaston	E	Private	Private
H.	Thominson	E	Private	Private
Bryant	Thompson	H	Private	Private
Emsley	Thompson	G	Private	Private
Gaston	Thompson	H	Private	Private
Isaac	Thompson	H	Private	Private
Isaiah	Thompson	H	Private	Private

James	Thompson	F	Private	Private
Neill	Thompson	H	Private	Private
Oscar V.	Thompson	F&S	First Lieutenant	Assistant Surgeon
V. Oscar	Thompson	F&S	First Lieutenant	Assistant Surgeon
Washington	Thompson	F	Private	Private
William	Thompson	E	Private	Private
M.H.	Thomson	H	Private	Sergeant
H.	Thorinson	E	Private	Private
Leonard L.	Thorneburg	K	Private	Private
L. Lafayette	Thromburg	K	Private	Private
Leonard L.	Throneburg	K	Private	Private
William S.	Tindale	I	Private	Private
William S.	Tindall	I	Private	Private
George H.	Todd	A	Private	Private
William	Todd	A	Private	Private
William	Tompson	E	Private	Private
Levi	Trafenstadt	K	Private	Private
Levi	Traffenstedt	K	Private	Private
Levi	Traffinstedt	K	Private	Private
Levi	Traverse	K	Private	Private
Levi	Travinstedt	K	Private	Private
Levi	Travis	K	Private	Private
Rufus T.	Traxler	B	Private	Private
Robert Preston	Tray	G	Second Lieutenant	Captain
John W.	Trexler	A	Private	Private
Rufus	Trexler	B	Private	Private
George	Trotter	F	Private	Private
William	Troutman	K	Private	Private
M.M.	Troy	G	Private	Private
Robert Preston	Troy	G	Second Lieutenant	Captain
Thomas Settle	Troy	F&S	Sergeant	Second Lieutenant
John B.	Troy, Jr.	G	Private	Private
George	Trutter	F	Private	Private
Edmond	Tucker	F	Private	Corporal
George	Tucker	K	Private	Private
Henry	Tucker	F	Private	Private
J. Pinkney	Tucker	K	Private	Private
Jesse D.	Tucker	F&S	Private	Ordnance Sergeant
John D.	Tucker	C	Private	Private

Lemuel B.	Tucker	C	Private	Private
Leonard B.	Tucker	C	Private	Private
T.P.	Tucker	K	Private	Private
George W.	Tunstall	C	Private	Private
Thomas R.	Tunstall	C	Private	Private
Henry	Turner	C	Private	Private
John J.	Turner	G	Corporal	Sergeant
Richard H.	Turner	C	Private	Private
Thomas	Turner	I	Private	Private
Robert	Upton	B	Private	Private
T.	Upton	B	Private	Private
D.Washington	Usry	E	Private	Private
Daniel W.	Usry	E	Private	Private
Freeman	Usry	E	Private	Corporal
J.Freeman	Usry	E	Private	Corporal
M.J.	Vallandigham	C	Private	Private
M.J.	Vanlandigham	C	Private	Private
Henry	Vann	I	Private	Private
Amos	Varner	G	Private	Private
Jesse	Varner	G	Private	Private
John G.	Varner	G	Private	Private
Nathan	Varner	G	Private	Private
N.C.	Verner	G	Private	Private
Henry	Vuncannon	F	Private	Private
John M.	Waddell	C	Sergeant	Second Lieutenant
John M.	Waddill	C	Sergeant	Second Lieutenant
William J.	Wadsworth	H	Private	Private
Christian A.	Waggoner	B	Private	Private
C.A.	Wagoner	B	Private	Private
William	Walder	A	Private	Corporal
Elisha	Walker	K	Private	Private
John J.	Walker	E	Private	First Lieutenant
Thomas P.	Walker	C	Private	Private
William	Walker	A	Private	Corporal
Robert	Wall	F	Private	Private
James	Wallace	D	Private	Private
Jesse L.	Wallace	B	Private	Private
Robert	Wallace	I	Private	Private
Washington	Wallace	D	Private	Private
William	Wallace	A	Private	Private

William	Wallace	D,I	Private	Private
Frederick	Waller	B	Private	Private
George	Waller	B	Private	Private
Jacob	Waller	B	Private	Private
John	Waller	B	Private	Private
William	Waller	A	Private	Corporal
J.L.	Wallis	B	Private	Private
James	Wallis	D	Private	Private
William	Wallis	D,I	Private	Private
T.	Walters	F	Private	
Thomas	Walters	D	Private	Private
B.F.	Walton	B	Private	Private
B.T.	Walton	B	Private	Private
Benjamin	Ward	G	Private	Private
Benjamin F.	Ward	A	Private	Private
Burrill	Warren	I	Private	Corporal
Burwell	Warren	I	Private	Corporal
Archibald R.	Warwick	A	Private	Private
Joseph	Warwick	A	Private	Private
Ephraim	Washington	E	Private	Private
Arthur	Waters	D	Private	Private
David	Waters	D	Private	Private
John	Waters	D	Private	Private
Thomas	Waters	D	Private	Private
Madison H.	Watkins	C	Private	Corporal
William	Watkins	G	Private	Private
Alexander M.	Watson	D	Private	Private
James S.	Watson	D	Private	Corporal
John H.	Watson	D	Private	Private
David	Watters	D	Private	Private
John	Watts	K	Private	Private
A. Don	Weaver	E	Private	Private
Atkinson D.	Weaver	E	Private	Private
Frederick	Weaver	K	Private	Private
George M.	Weaver	B	Private	Private
Henry	Weaver	K	Private	Private
Isaac	Weaver	E	Private	Private
Joseph	Weaver	E	Private	Private
M.	Weaver	B	Private	Private
W.	Weaver	B	Private	Private

Samuel P.	Weir Jr.	F	Second Lieutenant	Second Lieutenant
Andrew	West	A	Private	Private
G. S.	West		Surgeon	Surgeon
James	West	A	Private	Private
Middleton E.	West	A	Private	Private
Thomas Upton	West	B	Private	Private
James T.	Wheeler	E	Second Lieutenant	Second Lieutenant
John T.	Wheeler	E	Private	Sergeant
John Y.	Wheeler	E	Private	Sergeant
W. L.	Wheeler	E	Private	Private
Harmon	White	I	Private	Private
James A.	White	H	Private	Private
James C.	White	H	Private	Private
James E.	White	I	Private	Private
James J.	White	H	Private	Private
Oliver P.	White	I	First Lieutenant	First Lieutenant
George L.	Whitemer	K	Private	Private
Leander M.	Whitemer	K	Private	Private
Logan G.	Whitemer	K	Private	Private
George L.	Whitener	K	Private	Private
Leander M.	Whitener	K	Private	Private
Logan G.	Whitener	K	Private	Private
George L.	Whitner	K	Private	Private
L. G.	Whitner	K	Private	Private
Leander	Whitner	K	Private	Private
W. H. H.	Whitney	G	Private	Private
William H.	Whitney	G	Private	Private
Fred	Whitty	K	Private	Private
P.	Wice	B	Private	Private
John A.	Wicker	H	Private	Private
Kenneth	Wicker	H	Private	Private
Stephen	Wicker	H	Private	Private
John F.	Wike	K	Private	Private
Miles M.	Wike	K	Private	Private
William D.	Wike	K	Private	Private
George	Wilcox	H	Captain	Captain
James H.	Wilder		Private	Private
M. L.	Wilhelm	B	Private	Private
Allen	Wilkerson	A	Private	Private
Allen	Wilkerson	E	Private	Private

John A.	Wilkerson	E	Private	Private
Thomas M.	Wilkerson	E	Private	Private
Allen	Wilkinson	A	Private	Private
James A.	Wilkinson	D	Private	Private
T. M.	Wilkinson	E	Private	Private
Aaron	Willett	H	Private	Private
H. E.	Willett		Private	Private
John C.	Willett	H	Private	Private
W. L.	Willhelm	B	Private	Private
Franklin	Williams	A	Private	Corporal
M.	Williams	B	Private	Private
William M.	Williams	G	Private	Private
Allen	Williamson	I	Musician	Private
Isaac	Williamson	H	Private	Private
J.	Williamson	D	Private	Private
John	Williamson	·D	Private	Private
John F.	Williamson	F	Private	Private
W. S.	Williamson	E	Private	Private
David	Wilson	K	Private	Private
George W.	Wilson	K	Private	Private
James Lawson	Wilson	K	Private	Private
Martin	Wilson	D	Private	Private
Matthew M.	Wilson	K	Sergeant	Sergeant
Riley G.	Wilson	G	Private	Private
Marion	Winningham	G	Private	Private
S. T. Marion	Winningham	G	Private	Private
Benjamin	Wise	B	Private	Private
Pleasant	Wise	B	Private	Private
Francis M.	Wishart	A,B	First Lieutenant	Captain
John P.	Wishart	A	Private	Sergeant
Wellington	Wishart	A	Second Lieutenant	Second Lieutenant
August	Witherspoon	K	Private	Private
Augustus H.	Witherspoon	K	Private	Private
H. A.	Witherspoon	K	Private	Private
B. J.	Wood	B	Private	Private
Harris	Woodard	D	Private	Private
Hinson	Woodard	D	Private	Private
Lewis	Woodard	D	Private	Private
Louis	Wooddall	D	Private	Private
Burgess H.	Woods	B	Private	Private

J. B.	Woods	B	Private	Private
William	Woods	E	Private	Private
Henry J. K.	Workman	K	Private	Private
A. S.	Wright	G	Private	Private
Eli	Wright	G	Private	Private
H. P.	Wright	D	Private	Private
James	Wright	D	Private	Private
John C.	Wright	I	Sergeant	Second Lieutenant
Spinks	Wright	G	Private	Private
T. H.	Wright	H	Private	Sergeant Major
Thomas H.	Wright	H	Private	Sergeant Major
W. B.	Wright	E	Private	Private
R. R.	Wyatt	B	Private	Private
Roland H.	Wyatt	A	Private	Private
Wilson M. J.	Wyatt	B	Private	Private
William	Wycke	K	Private	Private
Andrew J.	Wynn	C	Private	Private
Peter	Wynn	C	Private	Private
Benjamin	Wyse	B	Private	Private
Pleasant	Wyse	B	Private	Private
N.	Yates	F	Private	Private
John A.	Yeates	G	Private	Private
Frederick L.	Yeats	F	Private	Private
Noah	Yeats	F	Private	Private
Peter R.	Yeats	F	Private	Private
Marcus	Yoder	K	Drummer	Musician
T. Clarkson	York	G	Private	Private
Thomas C.	York	G	Private	Private
Christ	Yost	F	Private	Private
Christopher	Yow	F	Private	Private
James	Yow	F	Private	Private
William	Yow	F	Private	Private
George	Yow, Jr.	F	Private	Private
George	Yow, Sr.	F	Private	Private

LIST OF MAPS

M-1. State of North Carolina, 1860
   (Manabin; North Carolina State Troops, 1861-1865)

M-2. Central Virginia and the City of Richmond, 1862

M-3. The Battle of Malvern Hill, Virginia 1862
   (The Seven Days Battles)

M-4. Sharpsburg, Maryland 1862

M-5. Fredericksburg, Virginia 1862-63

M-6. Bristoe Station, Virginia 1863

M-7. The Battle of the Wilderness, Virginia 1864

M-8. Spotsylania, Virginia 1864

M-9. The Battle of Cold Harbor, Virginia 1864

M-10. The Battle Line for Richmond, 1864

M-11. The Battle Line for Petersburg, 1864-5

M-12. Appromattox, Virginia, 1865

M-13. The Railroads of the Confederate States, 1861
   (Wiley, Bell I.; The Embattled Confederates; 1964)

LIST OF TABLES
&
ILLUSTRATIONS

ORDER OF BATTLE—CONFEDERATE FORCES

GENERAL FOOTNOTES

Chapter I - XVI.

1. Complied Service Records of Confederate Soldiers Who Served in Organization from the State of North Carolina; National Archives Microfilm Pubs, Microcopy; National Archives and Records Service, GSA, Washington, DC; 1959.

2. Manarin, Louis H. and Jordan, Weymonth T. Jr.; North Carolina State Troops 1861-1865; North Carolina Department of Archives and History, Raleigh, NC; 1987.

3. Confederate Military History—North Carolina; 12 Volumes; Confederate Publishing Company, Atlanta, GA; 1899; Volume 4.

4. War of the Rebellion: Official Records of Union and Confederate Armies. Published by the War Department, Washington, DC; 1881-1900.

5. Freeman, Douglas S.; Lee's Lieutenants;

6. Sprunt, James; Chronicles of the Cape Fear River; Reprint Company, Spartanburg, SC; 1973 c1916.

7. Confederate North Carolina Troops: 46th Regiment North Carolina Infantry; Civil War Database, National Parks Service, National Archives and Records Center, GSA, Washington, DC.

Battle Maps and Confederate Order of Battle:

8. McPherson, James A.; The Atlas of the Civil War; A Prentice-Hall Macmillan Company, New York, NY; 1994.

BIBLIOGRAPHY

A

Arms and Equipment of the Confederacy, Time-Life Book, Alexandra, VA; 1996.

B

Boatner, Mark M.; The Civil War Dictionary; David McKay Co. Inc. (Van Press), New York, NY; 1959.

C

Complied Service Records of Confederate Soldiers Who Served in Organizations from the State of North Carolina; National Archives Microfilm Pubs, Microcopy; National Archives and Records Service, GSA; Washington, DC; 1959.

Confederate Military History, North Carolina; 12 Volumes; Confederate Publishing Co., Atlanta, GA; 1899; Volume 4.

Confederate North Carolina Troops—2nd-7th-46th Regiment North Carolina Infantry; National Archives and Records Center, National Parks Service, Civil War Database; Washington, DC; 2006.

Confederate Veteran; "Edward D. Hall of North Carolina," Volume 4, No 7; Nashville, TN; July 1896.

D

E

F

Flato, Charles; The Golden Book of the Civil War; Golden Press, NY; 1961.

Freeman, Douglas Southall; Lee's Lieutenants; Charles Scribners Son's, New York, NY; 1971 (1943).

Freeman, Douglas Southall; R. E. Lee; Charles Scribners Son's, New York, NY; 1934.

G

Greenwell, Dale; The Third Mississippi Regiment—C.S.A.; Lewis Printing Service; Pascagoula, MS; 1972.

H

Howell, Andrew J.; The Book of Wilmington, Wilmington Printing, NC; 1930.

I

Illustrated Atlas of the Civil War, Time-Life Book; Alexandra, VA; 1996.

J

K

Krick, Robert K.; Lee's Colonels (biographical register), Morningside Press, Dayton, OH; 1992.

L

Lee, Fitzhugh; Confederate Soldier in the Civil War; The Fairfax Press (Crown Publishers), VA; 1895.

M

Manarin, Louis H. and Jordan, Weymonth T. Jr.; North Carolina State Troops 1861-1865, Volume 1-3; NC Department of Archives and History, Raleigh; Reprinted by Broadfoot Publishers Company, Wilmington, NC; (1987) 1988.

McPherson, James M.; The Atlas of the Civil War; A Prentice-Hall Macmillan Company, New York, NY; 1994.

N

North Carolina Military Organizations serving in the Civil War; University of North Carolina-Chapel Hill, Raleigh, NC; Undated.

O

Office of the Adjutant General, State of North Carolina; Register of Commissions, Raleigh, NC; 1861-1865.

P

Q

R

Robertson Jr., James I. and Kunstler, Mort; The Confederate Spirit, Rutledge Hill Press, Nashville, TN; 2000.

S

?? Sifakis, Stewart; Compendium of the Confederate Armies—North Carolina; Facts on File, Inc.; New York, NY; 1995.

Sprunt, James; Chronicles of the Cape Fear River; Reprint Company, Spartanburg, SC; 1973 c1916.

T

U

V

W

War of the Rebellion: Official Records of the Union and Confederate Armies. Published by the War Department, Washington, D.C.: 1881-1900.

Warner, Ezra J.; General's in Gray, Louisiana State University Press, Baton Rough, LA; 1987.

Wiley, Bell I.; The Embattled Confederates, Harper & Roe Company, New York, NY; 1964.

Woodworth, Steven E. and Winkle, Kenneth J.; Foreword by McPherson, James M.; Atlas of the Civil War, Oxford University Press, New York, NY; 2004.

X-Y-Z

THE RAILROADS OF THE CONFEDERATE STATES, 1861

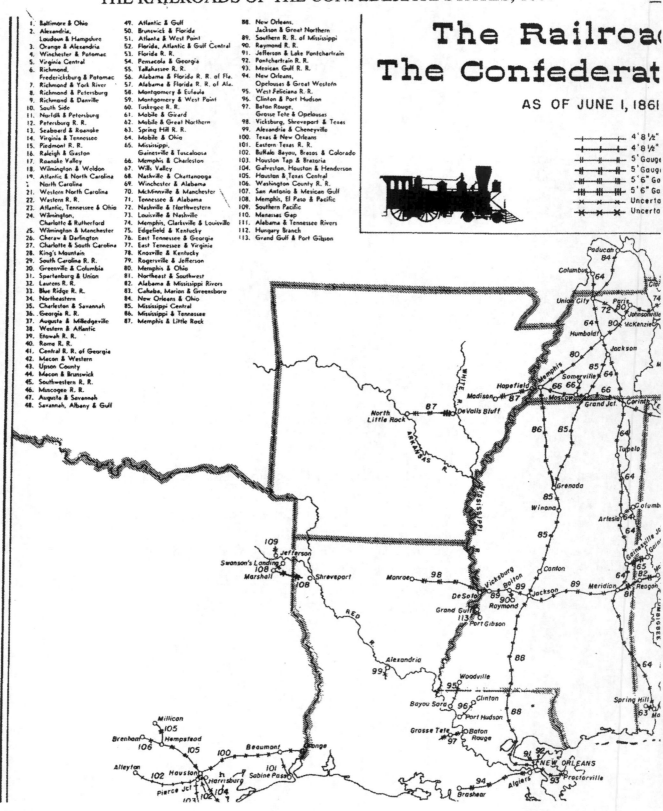

1. Baltimore & Ohio
2. Alexandria, Loudoun & Hampshire
3. Orange & Alexandria
4. Winchester & Potomac
5. Virginia Central
6. Richmond, Fredericksburg & Potomac
7. Richmond & York River
8. Richmond & Petersburg
9. Richmond & Danville
10. South Side
11. Norfolk & Petersburg
12. Petersburg R. R.
13. Seaboard & Roanoke
14. Virginia & Tennessee
15. Piedmont R. R.
16. Raleigh & Gaston
17. Roanoke Valley
18. Wilmington & Weldon
19. Atlantic & North Carolina
20. North Carolina
21. Western North Carolina
22. Western R. R.
23. Atlantic, Tennessee & Ohio
24. Wilmington, Charlotte & Rutherford
25. Wilmington & Manchester
26. Cheraw & Darlington
27. Charlotte & South Carolina
28. King's Mountain
29. South Carolina R. R.
30. Greenville & Columbia
31. Spartanburg & Union
32. Laurens R. R.
33. Blue Ridge R. R.
34. Northeastern
35. Charleston & Savannah
36. Georgia R. R.
37. Augusta & Milledgeville
38. Western & Atlantic
39. Etowah R. R.
40. Rome R. R.
41. Central R. R. of Georgia
42. Macon & Western
43. Upson County
44. Macon & Brunswick
45. Southwestern R. R.
46. Muscogee R. R.
47. Augusta & Savannah
48. Savannah, Albany & Gulf

49. Atlantic & Gulf
50. Brunswick & Florida
51. Atlanta & West Point
52. Florida, Atlantic & Gulf Central
53. Florida R. R.
54. Pensacola & Georgia
55. Tallahassee R. R.
56. Alabama & Florida R. R. of Fla.
57. Alabama & Florida R. R. of Ala.
58. Montgomery & Eufaula
59. Montgomery & West Point
60. Tuskegee R. R.
61. Mobile & Girard
62. Mobile & Great Northern
63. Spring Hill R. R.
64. Mobile & Ohio
65. Mississippi, Gainesville & Tuscaloosa
66. Memphis & Charleston
67. Wills Valley
68. Nashville & Chattanooga
69. Winchester & Alabama
70. McMinnville & Manchester
71. Tennessee & Alabama
72. Nashville & Northwestern
73. Louisville & Nashville
74. Memphis, Clarksville & Louisville
75. Edgefield & Kentucky
76. East Tennessee & Georgia
77. East Tennessee & Virginia
78. Knoxville & Kentucky
79. Rogersville & Jefferson
80. Memphis & Ohio
81. Northeast & Southwest
82. Alabama & Mississippi Rivers
83. Cahaba, Marion & Greensboro
84. New Orleans & Ohio
85. Mississippi Central
86. Mississippi & Tennessee
87. Memphis & Little Rock

88. New Orleans, Jackson & Great Northern
89. Southern R. R. of Mississippi
90. Raymond R. R.
91. Jefferson & Lake Pontchartrain
92. Pontchartrain R. R.
93. Mexican Gulf R. R.
94. New Orleans, Opelousas & Great Western
95. West Feliciana R. R.
96. Clinton & Port Hudson
97. Baton Rouge, Grosse Tete & Opelousas
98. Vicksburg, Shreveport & Texas
99. Alexandria & Cheneyville
100. Texas & New Orleans
101. Eastern Texas R. R.
102. Buffalo Bayou, Brazos & Colorado
103. Houston Tap & Brazoria
104. Galveston, Houston & Henderson
105. Houston & Texas Central
106. Washington County R. R.
107. San Antonio & Mexican Gulf
108. Memphis, El Paso & Pacific
109. Southern Pacific
110. Manasas Gap
111. Alabama & Tennessee Rivers
112. Hungary Branch
113. Grand Gulf & Port Gibson

The Railroa
The Confederat
AS OF JUNE 1, 1861

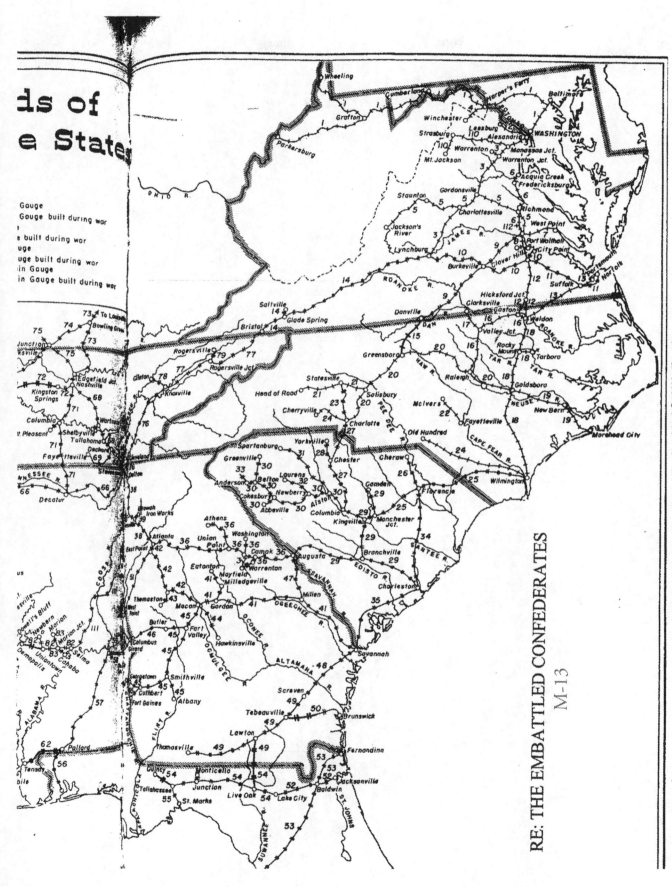

RE: THE EMBATTLED CONFEDERATES
M-13

"BOOKS TO BULLETS"
In defiance of Northern Propaganda!

Complied & Edited by
COL Charles W.L. Hall

A History of the
46th NORTH CAROLINA INFANTRY, C.S.A.

Over 2,000 men were recruited for this regiment from the counties of Robeson, Rowan, Warren, Richmond, Granville, Moore, Randolph, Sampson and Catawba, throughout 1861-1865! The 46th North Carolina persevered over three years of unbelievable hardship - valorously, and under the constant threat of death! Honoring all North Carolinian's past and present! Part of the real life story is given to us, through the memoirs and diary of Brigadier General Edward Dudley Hall, Commanding Cooke's Brigade, ANV of Wilmington, New Hanover County. Every attempt has been made to fully represent our regiment in this book, to include a Regimental Roster of all officers and men who selflessly served their state, their conscience and the Confederacy!

Currently available as a pre-publication promotion! Sale in soft cover $49.95 +S&H, hardcover $75.00 +S&H. When ordered direct from publisher, will ship in 6-8 weeks. To order: Attn: Confederate Press, New Horizons Development Company. P.O. Box 15171, Hattiesburg, MS 39404-1517

135